# GREAT
# LEADERSHIP
# IDEAS

## FROM SUCCESSFUL LEADERS AND
## MANAGERS AROUND THE WORLD

### Jonathan Gifford

**Marshall Cavendish**
Business

# CONTENTS

## The ideas

## Part 4 – You And The Organization

## Part 5 – Personal Qualities

## Part 6 – Personal Behavior

## Part 7 – Personal Development

## Part 8 – You And The Outside World

# ACKNOWLEDGEMENTS

ALL OF THE ideas in this book are illustrated by direct quotations from leaders—collected from books, articles, published interviews and websites. I would like to thank every leader whose thoughts and comments have been used to bring life to theoretical notions and to offer practical illustrations as to how these leadership ideas might be put into practice.

Some leaders feature on more occasions than others—typically because they have written valuable autobiographies or accounts of their business experience that offer a wealth of material. Jack Welch of General Electric, Lee Iacocca of Chrysler, Richard Branson of Virgin Group, David Packard of Hewlett-Packard and Louis Gerstner of IBM all fit into this category, as does a figure from an earlier generation—and a firm favourite of mine—Sir John Harvey-Jones of ICI.

The ideas of several distinguished business academics also feature here—particularly those of John P. Kotter, Gary Hamel and Michael Beers, all from Harvard Business School.

The mentor, business coach and writer, Marshall Goldsmith, is so insightful about the elements of personal behavior that can so easily hamper (or encourage) the effectiveness of senior executives that it is almost impossible not to quote Goldsmith on matters of personal behavior.

Alan Leighton must be singled out for special acknowledgement. His book *On Leadership* not only offers typically pragmatic and insightful advice based on Leighton's own management style, it also provides useful and pertinent comment from a wide range of contemporary leaders, several of whom are quoted here from Leighton.

I would like, again, to thank all of the 133 leaders whose comments were used in the writing of this book. References to all books, articles and websites from which quotes were obtained can be found in Sources.

Finally, I would like to thank Martin Liu, of Marshall Cavendish International, for his support, encouragement and advice; also Martin's colleagues in London and Singapore.

# INTRODUCTION

It is very easy to be a successful leader. All you need is the charisma of a hero; the wisdom of a philosopher; the vision of a seer; the interpersonal skills of a diplomat; the memory of an elephant; the stamina and fitness of an athlete; the integrity of a judge; the presentation skills of an actor; the humility of a saint; the confidence of a politician ...

Drawing up a list of all the skills, attributes and characteristics that a modern leader needs was an easy task. I have a list of at least a further one hundred attributes that were not included in this book. So much is required of the ideal leader—so many ideal personal qualities; so many behavioral skills!

Nevertheless, selecting which leadership "ideas" should actually feature in the book was also, in the end, a relatively simple task. I began to build a database of quotations from real leaders, illustrating real leadership issues, and to file them under headings like the ones featured in this book: Have a Vision; Make it Happen; Seek out Change; Allow Choice to Drive Decisions; Be demanding; Be Fair; Set reasonable Goals ... so far, so simple.

As the database began to grow, noteworthy quotations from real leaders began to cluster around certain topics. In a very real sense, the "ideas" featured in this book have been dictated by the real observations of well over one hundred leaders. If few leaders had anything of real interest to say about a particular topic that had seemed relevant, it fell off the list. If leader after leader had something valuable to say about a particular area, it not only stayed in, but was also on occasions subdivided into more specific ideas.

One of the most fundamental ideas featured in this book is one that is perhaps best set out by Harvard Business School Professor, John Kotter. It is the deceptively simple notion that leadership is all about change, whereas management, in sharp contrast, is all about stasis. Management is about perfecting a known process; it hates surprises; it aims for perfection. Leadership is about change and risk—about uncertainty and leaps into the unknown. Management can motivate people by the usual rewards and censures. Leadership can only succeed by inspiring people. Nobody undertakes significant upheaval until they have been persuaded of the need for change at some quite fundamental, emotional level. Leaders have to persuade. Nobody can lead without followers.

It cannot be a coincidence that the most heavily populated areas of my database of quotations have to do with innovation; with change; with creativity. This is the very stuff of leadership.

It is also no coincidence that the other major theme to emerge was one that might be put under the heading of "market forces" or "natural selection"—or, perhaps, of "democracy".

Leaders are leaders of teams. Leaders themselves, despite their apparently astonishing abilities, are still only one person, with one brain and one set of ideas. The organization has many people, with many brains and many more ideas. All of these people are focused on the same ends; they work in the same field; they know the same markets and share the same knowledge-base. They share common objectives and significant comradeship. They have new ideas and untapped funds of creativity; they are keen to contribute.

The collective wisdom of the organization can be the key to a leader's success. So, potentially, can its adaptability. In numbers there is variety, and variety—of thought, of skills, of aptitudes, of ideas—is the key to survival. Leaders should be very wary of dictating what the future of the organization should be, and should be very focused on listening to what the organization itself believes to be the way forward.

Which brings us to the uncomfortable conclusion that much current management thinking is outmoded. We have touched on John Kotter's "deceptively simple" point that leadership is about change, while management is about sticking with what you know and refining an existing process to a point approaching perfection. Management knows exactly what needs to be done to achieve this; the organization will become more and more precisely focused on the set of skills needed to carry out its chosen tasks and to achieve its chosen goals. Where, in this system, is the search for innovation? Improvement, yes; but not innovation. Where is the drive to encourage colleagues to think laterally, to explore new options, to have wild and crazy ideas (some of which might just work)? Where is the encouragement of the diversity that will help the organization to adapt to changing conditions? The perfectly-managed process will, quite intentionally, drive all variation and diversity out of the system.

It is an interesting challenge for a leader—the central challenge. How do you encourage creative and entrepreneurial thinking within an organization, while still managing that organization to produce goods and services at a level of efficiency that can compete in the global market?

These ideas are not new. Kotter wrote *A Force for Change* in 1990, expanding his theory of the centrality of change to leadership, and of the need for leaders to recognize the difference, in themselves and in their team, between leadership and management skills—and also to recognize when each particular skill was needed. Management without leadership is very unlikely to achieve change. Leadership without management is likely to produce chaos.

Gary Hamel wrote *The Future of Management* in 1997. In this book, Hamel challenges leaders of modern organizations to give up some of their traditional powers; to offer colleagues a degree of freedom of choice as to what projects they pursue, for example, and to allow these internal "market forces" to allow resources to follow these choices; to devolve decision-making as far down the line and as close to the customer as possible.

In my experience, these things are still not happening in most companies. There are a few shining examples, but they seem to be the exception and not the rule. We are, understandably, wedded to the old military "command and control" model that was quite deliberately adopted by the management of the earliest major corporations, created in the late nineteenth and early twentieth centuries. In this model, the leader is king or queen (or commander-in-chief). Commands cascade down the pyramid of management. People jump to. "Yes, sir" or "Yes, Ma'am" is the correct response.

Will this work for much longer, I wonder, when talented people are less convinced of the need to sign their freedoms away in exchange for a salary, uncertain job security and an unexceptional pension?

If leadership is about change, then leadership must itself embrace change. I came away from writing this book with an even greater conviction that the successful organizations of the twenty-first century will be led in a very different way. The key words in a modern leader's lexicon will be words like these: consensual; collaborative; empowering; devolved; consultative; inspirational.

*

This book is divided into sections, in order to allow ideas to gather together around core leadership themes.

"Vision, Mission, Values, Change" is a relatively short summary of current thinking about these concepts. You need to get your vision distinguished from your mission and to set in train your programme of change. It is interesting how many successful leaders stress that you can agonize too much about this stage: "get on and do it" is their message: make it happen; implement. Your competitors also have good ideas and clever strategies, but the leader who implements most effectively will win. The core question of "values" is different. Having the right values in place and fully understood by the whole team will guarantee the quality of the relationship between the organization and its clients, and help to steer the organization through difficult times. Organizations that lack core values tend to unravel, as individuals put their own interests before those of their colleagues.

"You and the Top Team" is straightforward but central. You can't do everything yourself: build a well-balanced top team; don't be afraid to recruit to your weaknesses; avoid building a team of people "just like you". You need strength in depth, and you need a variety of skills and attitudes to help shape corporate policy.

"You and the Whole Team" investigates your relationship with all of your colleagues. Communication and engagement feature prominently, as do devolution, honest relationships and empowerment.

"You and the Organization" looks at the more formal aspects of your leadership: about making structural changes that will help the organization to help itself. Some of the most significant chapters in the book (in my opinion) are in this section: "Create an entrepreneurial culture"; "Encourage diversity"; "Encourage innovation"; "Harness the intelligence of the organization"; "March towards the sound of the guns"; "Mix things up"; "Practice democracy".

"Personal Qualities" and "Personal behavior" come next. This is the finger-wagging bit (for which I apologize). Be firm! Be passionate! Be authentic! Say sorry! It's tough on you, but it is essential. As the business coach and mentor, Marshall Goldsmith points out, at this stage in your career, about the only thing you can hope to really change about yourself is your personal behavior, since your other skill-sets are pretty much in place. Changing your behavior towards your colleagues is also, happily, the one thing that is most likely to improve your chances of success.

"Personal Development" is a bit more relaxing. Some of it is even quite indulgent: get yourself a really good PA; cut out unnecessary distractions; make life easier and more efficient by managing your time really well. But you can't escape from the admonishments, even here. Get fit! Learn from failure! Recognize people! I apologize again, in advance—but you know it makes sense.

Finally, "You and the Outside World" looks at your relationship with the big wide world out there. We are finally understanding that even for-profit companies are not merely machines for making money. Successful organizations have a purpose that goes beyond making money. Making profit is the starting point; it justifies your use of capital. "Making a contribution" is far more important, as is "Doing the right thing".

As the leader, you have to make sure that your organization "does the right thing". There have been several significant examples of recent leaders who have failed to do the right thing, either by their organization or by the outside world. It is important for all of us that the leaders of the future do not fail us all in this way.

It's a tough job, and you can only give it your best shot. I hope that you succeed, and I hope that this book helps in some measure, by offering the advice and guidance of many leaders who have gone before you.

Good luck!

# PART 1
# MISSION, VISION, VALUES, CHANGE

# HAVE A VISION

---

A VISION SETS out a view of what the organization should look like in the future and of the way in which it will have changed the world. A really successful vision will inspire an organization, and affect every decision that is taken.

---

## The idea

The Wal-Mart Stores retail group is one of the world's largest public corporations in terms of revenue. The founder, Sam Walton, said, "If we work together, we'll lower the cost of living for everyone ... we'll give the world an opportunity to see what it's like to save and have a better life."

"Saving people money to help people live better" is still the company's vision. The vision of Microsoft Corporation is "To help people and businesses throughout the world to realize their full potential". Google's vision is "To organize the world's information and make it universally accessible and useful". Nike aims "To bring inspiration and innovation to every athlete in the world".

A vision should be specific enough to guide people's future behavior, but sufficiently general to allow for changing circumstances, and to allow the organization to use its initiative in deciding how best to achieve the vision.

Some visions are apparently stark and simple and need to be "unpacked" to reveal all of the organization's values but, in the best examples, all of these values are implied in a simple, bold statement.

Wu Xiaobing, president and MD of pharmaceutical company Wyeth China, says, "To me, the most important thing for a leader is to create a vision and get everyone on the management team to believe, be convinced and excited and work for that. In most cases, if there is a vision, people will work hard together to create a miracle. If you are only dealing with daily business, and even if you are busy every day, you won't go very far and you won't have breakthrough. The leader must have a good vision, and then people will become inspired." The corporate vision of Wyeth is "To be the world's best pharmaceutical company". It unpacks this vision to reveal the goal of "developing innovative new medicines that really make a difference to people's lives and address significant areas of unmet medical need."

## In practice

- A vision sets out a future that the organization seeks to bring about. It is a statement of where the organization hopes to get to, what it aspires to be and what change it intends to bring into people's lives.

- A vision should be simple and bold; it is not a definition of the organization's role—this is set out in the mission statement.

- The vision should inspire the organization, give it purpose and act as a reference point for every decision. It should persist through changing circumstances and different strategies.

# ESTABLISH YOUR MISSION

THE ORGANIZATION'S MISSION statement is different from the leader's vision, which is a view of how the ideal future would look. The mission statement is about the present; about what the organization does, for whom and why. When it is well defined and clearly presented, the mission can be as inspiring as the vision: it gives people clear and immediate goals and targets.

## The idea

Jack Welch, chairman and CEO of General Electric from 1981 to 2001, defines the ideal mission statement with characteristic force.

"In my experience, an effective mission statement basically answers one question: How do we intend to win in this business? ... It requires companies to make choices about people, investment, and other resources, and it prevents them from falling into the common mission trap of asserting they will be all things to all people at all times ... Effective mission statements balance the possible and the impossible. They give people a clear sense of the direction to profitability and the inspiration to feel they are part of something big and important. Take our mission at GE as an example. From 1981 through 1995, we said we were going to be 'the most competitive enterprise in the world' by being No. 1 or No. 2 in every market—fixing, selling, or closing every underperforming business that couldn't get there."

There could be no doubt about what this mission statement meant or entailed. It was specific, descriptive, with nothing abstract going on. And it was inspirational too, in its global ambition. General Electric's vision was "To be the most competitive enterprise in the world". Its mission was "To be No. 1 or No. 2 in every market".

John Mackey, co-founder and CEO of the USA's natural and organic foods retailer, Whole Foods Market, says this about his company's mission:

"The business has a mission or deeper purpose beyond maximizing profits to the shareholders ... Our mission is ... to sell the highest quality natural, organic foods in the world. And that's our deepest mission. And then we organize our stakeholders around that mission, satisfying the customers, team-member happiness and excellence, increasing shareholder value through profits and through growth and taking care of the communities and the environment ... we're mission-driven in that we try to fulfil those core values which include, but go beyond, simply maximizing profits."

Whole Food's *vision* is encapsulated in its motto: "Whole foods, whole people, whole planet".

## In practice

- Vision is about the relatively distant future; mission is about the present.

- A mission statement spells out what the organization offers, to whom and why, and how it intends to achieve that mission.

- A clear mission statement is inspiring in itself, since it sets out clearly what the organization will do and how. It sets clear goals for the team.

# ESTABLISH YOUR VALUES

An organization needs a vision and a strategy, but it also needs a value system. These values will affect every aspect of corporate culture, and can ensure that every employee understands how he or she is expected to behave in any circumstance.

## The idea

The Texas-based American low-cost airline, Southwest, established itself on a platform of exceptional customer service. Its former president, Colleen Barrett, explains how the company's values are nailed to its mast: "Our mission statement is posted every three feet, all over every location that we have, so if you're a customer, you've seen it. It's to follow the Golden Rule—to treat people the way that you want to be treated, and pretty much everything will fall into place." Every employee needs to be able to take this fundamental approach to heart, says Barrett: "We hire for attitude and we train for skill, and we are far more likely to terminate someone for attitude and behavior and lack of respect than just about anything else."

Dieter Zetsche, chairman of Daimler AG and head of Mercedes Benz Cars, highlights four values that form the heart of the company's culture: passion, respect, integrity and discipline. Every Daimler employee must have a passion for cars; respect must encompass customers, colleagues, business partners and shareholders; integrity dictates that every employee anywhere in the world adheres to the highest ethical standards. The fourth value is discipline.

"When we talk about discipline," says Zetsche, "what we mean is the ability to choose the truth over convenience."

Subroto Bagchi is a co-founder of MindTree, a global IT solutions consultancy with headquarters in Bangalore, India, and New Jersey, USA. The young company asked its employees to choose the values that would define the organization. Now, says Bagchi, the company places alignment with its core values first in its recruitment and appraisal policies.

"The responses were synthesized into five key values. These are Caring, Learning, Achieving, Sharing, and Social Sensitivity. We now find that these have been internalized. These have been embedded into our performance management system and our recruitment system. We certainly believe that value alignment precedes competence. The world is full of competent people ... If values are in place, competence can always be developed."

## In practice

- An organization's values usually emerge naturally from its original vision, but the team needs to explore these values so that they are clear to all.

- The values must be widely publicized; managers must work hard to ensure that they have been understood by everyone in the organization.

- A lapse in behavior by any member of the team can be surprisingly damaging; a team that has internalized the values can be trusted to behave in the best interests of the organization in every situation.

- Alignment with the organization's values is of primary importance in recruitment and promotion: skills can be taught; not everyone has the right attitude.

# MAKE IT HAPPEN

ALL OF A leader's great plans come to nothing if they are not successfully executed. Leaders make things happen.

## The idea

Michael Eisner, former CEO of the Walt Disney Company, now runs the privately held investment company Tornante.

As Eisner says about execution, "The problem is not the ideas, the problem is getting them executed. And I don't or cannot remember a successful movie or television show that we've ever made that I didn't get many letters saying, 'That was my idea,' or 'Oh you did a movie. It was just like something I was thinking about doing.' And what I want to say is, 'Well, why didn't you do it?' And the problem is that it is a big step from having an idea flow from out of your head, and getting it on a piece of paper, getting people around you to think it's a good idea, finding a writer, putting on a show—look how hard it is to put on a show in High School!"

Louis Gerstner, previous CEO of IBM, says that making it happen is possibly more important than developing a brilliant new strategy—which may, in any case, be highly risky. "Execution—getting the task done, making it happen—is the most unappreciated skill of an effective business leader. In my years as a consultant, I participated in the development of many strategies for many companies ... It is extremely difficult to develop a unique strategy for a company; and if the strategy is truly different, it is probably highly risky. The reason for this is that industries are defined and bound by economic models, explicit customer expectations, and competitive structures that are known to all and impossible to change in a short period of time ... So, execution really is the critical part of a successful strategy. Getting it done, getting it done right, getting it done better than the next person is far more important than dreaming up new visions of the future."

## In practice

- Many people have good ideas; few actually carry them out; fewer still carry them out with excellence.

- Businesses are constrained by well-known economic and market factors that limit the scope for truly original new strategies. Your competitors almost certainly have the same ideas that you do. The leader who executes those ideas most successfully—who makes things happen most effectively—wins.

# 5 SEEK OUT CHANGE

BRINGING ABOUT CHANGE is the primary function of leadership. Change is frightening because it is, by definition, a leap into the dark. However, change is unavoidable: market conditions can shift quite suddenly and with little or no warning.

Leaders must instil a sense of open-mindedness in the organization and encourage the team to explore new ideas.

## The idea

Harvard Business professor and author John Kotter writes: "Leadership produces change. That is its primary function." Leaders must set the direction for change, and Kotter points out that this is not the same as planning: "Planning is a management process ... primarily designed to help produce orderly results, not change." Making a change or coping with change is, by definition, risky. It takes us into unfamiliar territory where no established management processes can help us.

Richard Branson, chairman of Virgin Group, is frank about the fact that change is not welcome: "It's no good saying 'Prepare for change' or 'Embrace change' ... The bald fact is, change, most of the time, is a threat. It's the thing that wants to kill you. And let's face it: one day, it will." But Branson is proud of his own group's record: "What delights me is the way the company has continued to innovate its way out of trouble. A defensive, conservative, cautious mindset—a natural enough reaction when things get tough—can kill you stone dead in a competitive marketplace. When your existence is threatened, you have to change. This is one of the hardest lessons to learn in business, because it is so counter-intuitive."

# In practice

- Leadership is primarily about change and involves risk. The leader's function is to choose the right direction for change.

- The environment in which organizations operate can change quite suddenly. Leaders need to create an attitude throughout the organization that expects change and is willing to adapt.

- Leaders should encourage an environment of constant innovation. Organizations that actively seek out change are more likely to stay ahead of the game.

- When a change in the outside world takes the organization by surprise, internal change is essential. Keeping on doing the same thing will not work.

# PART 2
# YOU AND
# THE TOP TEAM

# 6 BUILD THE PERFECT TOP TEAM

THE TOP TEAM transforms the leader's ideas into action. It is easy for leaders to imagine that they should recruit a top team of people who are similar to themselves. The ideal top team is a healthy mix of attitudes and abilities.

## The idea

Leaders should actively "recruit to their weaknesses" and seek out people who are good at what they themselves are less good at. We all resist this, partly because we are afraid that the other person may succeed where we fail. We are also instinctively drawn to people who are like ourselves.

Daisy Poon built a food export business in China before looking for other business opportunities. During a trade visit to Japan, she was impressed by the Japanese Ajisen Noodle restaurant chain, whose meals also reminded her of the broth-based noodle dishes that her mother made when she was a child. She won the licence to develop the brand in China and opened her first restaurants in Hong Kong and then Shenzhen. The Ajisen Noodle chain is now one of China's leading fast-food chains.

"My view is that teamwork is fundamental. The people in your executive management team are very important. We have around four or five people on the team. One works on operations, one on finance, one on human resources management ... We have some disagreements in our work, but we try to complement each other ... Within the team, there has to be someone who can take the fight to the market place, someone who is tolerant and calm, someone who can keep things under control, and someone who thinks in greater detail. You have to have these different traits within one team, and the skill to organize all these people is crucial."

## In practice

- A leader is primarily a strategist and a decision maker. Most if not all implementation should be carried out by your team.

- Select your top team with great care; look for people with different skills and abilities who will complement you and each other.

- Self-confident leaders do not need to feel that they know all of the answers or that they are superior to the rest of the team. They are the team leader.

- The leader's job is to keep this team functioning smoothly and heading in the chosen direction; great diplomatic skills will be required.

- The top team will need to be constantly "upgraded" to meet new challenges—but if the team was chosen well, this will require advice, training and motivation rather than replacement.

# CHALLENGE THE MANAGEMENT STRUCTURE

EVERYONE TENDS TO take the management structure as given. We all work within the organization's structure and we tend to think that, of all the things that we can change, this structure is immutable.

Most organizational structures are very old fashioned: a pyramid with the leader at the top, the "management" in the middle and the "workers" at the bottom. Leaders can challenge this structure and experiment with new organizational models.

## The idea

Nick Yang, founder of the Chinese mobile internet company KongZhong, set up a senate-based management system copied from the Swiss system of government by council.

"I have 40 people working for me. I actually have a very innovative way of management. We have what we call the Senate. I told the company that we run a constitutional monarchy. There are certain things I decide. There are certain things the Senate decides. The Senate is a representation of the teams. Every 10 guys have one Senator. The Senate decides on things such as budgeting, salaries and compensations ... Some issues, such as, 'Where do we go for our spring trip?' or 'How do we spend our team-building budget?' are decided by the entire employee body. Other things are decided by the Senate. People are very involved and happy that they have such empowerment."

Zhang Ruimin is chairman and CEO of China's leading white-goods manufacturer Haier Group, where every department faces its own clients.

"Our first step has been to restructure the organization from a triangle pointing upwards to one pointing down. You put the clients at the top and then the line manager, employees and then the top leaders, who are now obliged to provide resources to the line managers, at the bottom. Every department has to face their own clients, becoming what we call 'autonomous units'. Teams have ownership of their revenue targets and are incentivized to deliver additional revenue. There are three advantages to this method. First is that responding to market demand doesn't take long. Line managers can make decisions on their own, with no need to wait for feedback from their superiors. Secondly, it solves the internal gaming issues. Everyone has their own market target and they have to align their own interests with that target to achieve a 'win-win' result."

## In practice

- Traditional "command and control" systems of management based on military models and adopted by the world's first major industrial concerns over a century ago are almost certainly not the systems that will be successful in the 21st century.

- Modern management thinking favors far more devolved management models that empower managers and colleagues, and give them ownership of their own budgets.

- You are the leader. There is no rule that says you have to continue with the old managerial structure. Be creative.

- Make sure that the organization is fanatically focused on its customers; try to give colleagues as much freedom as possible; allow key decisions to be taken as close to the customer as possible; think about ways of directly rewarding success.

# 8 COLLABORATE

LEADERS MUST COLLABORATE with their colleagues and work together with them to achieve the organization's goals. People are no longer motivated by the old hierarchical style of leadership; they need to be consulted and inspired.

## The idea

In the early days of industrialization, corporations looked to the military as the ideal model for an efficient corporate structure. Harvard Business School professor and business author, Bill George, looks back on his early days at Harvard.

"In my 1960s class at Harvard Business School, our professor cited the Department of Defense ... as the most iconic organization. Business followed their lead, as General Electric, General Motors, AT&T, and Sears became their role models. By century's end, the latter three were in long-term decline, while GE was revolutionized by Jack Welch. Hundreds of other organizations like Kodak, Motorola, and Westinghouse followed similar patterns of self-destruction. The hierarchical model simply wasn't working. In retrospect, it seems obvious people weren't responding to 'top-down' leadership."

Amongst other reasons for this shift, George cites the fact that today's knowledge-workers are less prepared to simply trade their time for money and to follow a set of instructions. They look to find satisfaction and meaning in their work, and expect a collaborative relationship with the organization.

Marten Hansen, management professor at the University of California, writes about the cultural change that has come about in what is expected in leadership style.

"Over the past 20 years we have lived in an era that has worshipped the managers as heroes that ride into town and make things great. They make the decisions, they call the shots, they are the geniuses. Now that one-star model is becoming outdated. We need collaborative leaders that harness the collective intelligence around them."

Leaders themselves must adopt a more collaborative style, but Hansen warns that collaboration throughout the organization must be focused.

"The goal of collaboration is not collaboration but better results. This means that you should only collaborate when it is the best way to improve performance; many times it is better to work independently." Hansen recommends that leaders carefully select which projects colleagues should collaborate on (and which not), that they understand the barriers that currently prevent employees from collaborating, and find management solutions that tear down those barriers.

## In practice

- A leader is the leader of a team. Working with a team involves real collaboration.

- Colleagues want to find satisfaction and meaning in their work. They need to be inspired and involved.

- The point of collaboration is to get better results. Not every project will benefit from collaboration—but most will.

- Look for structural issues that prevent colleagues from collaborating with each other.

# DELEGATE

ALL LEADERS HAVE a tendency to assume that they must personally find a solution to every new problem. While leaders will always be responsible for any outcome, they have to delegate the process that achieves that outcome. Successful delegation is a considerable skill.

The reverse side of delegation is the removal of decision-making powers from colleagues in an attempt to legislate against a repetition of past errors. This will not succeed and will begin to erode the organization's ability to think for itself.

## The idea

Successful delegation is a great skill: people who take on a task must understand clearly what is required of them, and by when; how their task fits into the organization's overall vision and what parameters they must work within. They must feel both responsible for their task and motivated to carry it out. Lee Iacocca, President and CEO of the USA's Chrysler Corporation in the 1980s, remembers learning about delegation: "You don't know how to delegate," said Iacocca's boss.

"Now don't get me wrong. You're the best guy I've got. Maybe you're even as good as two guys put together. But even so—that's still only two guys. You've got a hundred people working for you right now— what happens when you've got ten thousand?" Iacocca commented: "He taught me to stop trying to do everybody's job. And he taught me how to give other people a goal—and how to motivate them to achieve it. I've always felt that a manager has achieved a great deal when he's able to motivate one other person. When it comes to making a place run, motivation is everything."

John Harvey-Jones, ex-chairman of chemicals company ICI, makes a subtle point about the tendency of organizations to legislate against repeats of previous disasters—with the result that freedom of action is removed from executives.

"A business mistake is made, and it is assumed that the mistake would have been avoided if somebody at a higher position in the organization had known about it or had intervened ... A power that had been delegated previously is therefore removed, usually in quite a small way, by an instruction that in such and such a case the matter is to be referred upwards. Of course that exact case never occurs, or if it does, it occurs in such a way that it is not recognized as being a repeat run of the previous bitter experience. You therefore get an increasing tangle of bureaucratic instructions which seek to legislate for an endless series of unlikely events that have occurred at some time in the organization's past."

## In practice

- Leaders must delegate skillfully to their managers and inspire them to motivate their teams in turn.

- Removing managers' discretionary powers in an attempt to prevent repeats of previous errors is unlikely to work. Future situations never exactly repeat past circumstances, and leaders are no better placed to avoid mistakes than their senior team.

- Taking responsibility out of people's hands creates an atmosphere where the team tries to avoid breaking rules as opposed to trying to achieve goals.

# DEVOLVE DECISION MAKING

LEADERS SHOULD GO beyond delegating tasks and devolve actual decision making. Organizations in which key decisions are made by a few individuals at the top of the hierarchy rely entirely on the experience and judgement of those few people, on their ability to absorb what information is fed to them and on the quality of that information.

Devolving decision making to the level that is closest to the customer accesses the most accurate knowledge.

## The idea

Irene Rosenfeld, CEO and chairman of Kraft Food Inc, talks about how the food giant achieved success, especially in China, with its Oreo sandwich cookie—a billion dollar product in the USA—when they devolved key decisions to local managers.

"We began by giving the responsibility of making some of those decisions back to our local managers. In the past, we would have mandated what an Oreo looked like around the world from Northfield, Illinois. And that wasn't necessarily consistent with what consumers in the local markets were eating. So what we found was sandwich cookies as a format is just not appealing to Chinese consumers but wafer formats are what they are eating. And so all we did was take the flavoring and the strong cocoa taste of our Oreo together with some of the fabulous marketing that we've done around the world, and brought it to the Chinese consumer. And we are pleased to see that it is the fastest growing biscuit in China right now."

John Mackey is the co-founder and CEO of Whole Foods Market, the American retailer of natural and organic products.

The company has always believed in devolving as much decision-making power as possible. Each store is staffed by approximately eight teams of colleagues, which work as relatively independent units. Teams are free to buy locally and to choose which products they stock, following strict standards set by the centre. This gives each Whole Foods store a unique mix of products that suit local tastes and reflect local suppliers. Even recruitment decisions are devolved: new recruits join teams for a four-week trial period, after which the team votes as to whether they are taken on—a two-thirds majority is needed. The profit-per-labor-hour of every team is calculated every four weeks, and bonuses are awarded on these figures. Whole Foods teams have a good reason to accept only industrious new recruits.

## In practice

- Set objectives and allow the organization to propose the best means to achieve those objectives.

- Devolve decision making as far as possible to the level nearest to the consumer.

- Give teams the power to make their own decisions about things that affect performance and results. Give them the information they need to monitor their own performance, and reward them on the basis of results, in terms of both money and recognition.

# LEADER-MANAGERS

LEADERSHIP AND MANAGEMENT require very different outlooks and different skills. Leaders should distinguish carefully between the two and decide on the combination of leadership and management skills needed in their own role.

Organizations also require leader-managers at many different levels: any colleague, anywhere in the organization, may be called on to lead a project or an initiative.

## The idea

Harvard Business School professor and leadership writer, John Kotter, argues that whereas management is about perfecting an existing process, eliminating variation and risk, leadership is all about change, which inevitably involves risk. People can be "managed" to perform essential and routine tasks, but they will need to be *inspired* to set out on a different path with uncertain results.

As Kotter says, "Because they are called upon to produce expected results constantly, managerial processes must be as close as possible to fail-safe and risk-free. That in turn means they cannot be dependent on the unusual or hard to obtain ... Leadership is different. Achieving grand visions despite the obstacles always requires an occasional burst of energy, the kind that certain motivational and inspirational processes can provide. Such processes accomplish their energizing effect, not by pushing people in the right direction, as a control mechanism often does, but by satisfying very basic human needs: for achievement, belonging, recognition, self-esteem, a sense of control over one's life, and living up to one's ideals. These processes touch us deeply and powerfully, and elicit a most powerful response."

Kotter makes the point that different situations will require different mixes of leadership and management, and says that "leader-managers" are needed throughout the organization. An organization with strong leadership and weak management can easily run out of control, despite having a strong group culture and high levels of inspiration. Many entrepreneurial start-ups go wrong for this reason. Conversely, an organization that is strong on management and weak on leadership may try to manage its way through change, usually with disastrous results.

## In practice

- Management and leadership are very different things.

- Management seeks to make an established and successful process as efficient as possible; to eliminate variation and risk. Management of people tends to be approached in the same way, with a system of rewards and censures.

- Leadership is about change in order to achieve a new long-term vision for the organization. It inevitably involves risk.

- Leaders must inspire colleagues to embrace this process—the normal rewards for success or failure are unlikely to persuade colleagues to undertake a change programme.

- Colleagues will need to be motivated by one or several drivers that function at an emotional level, such as a sense of achievement, self-esteem and belonging.

- Leaders should be aware of the difference between leadership and management in their role and encourage senior colleagues to become "leader-managers", using leadership skills, when needed, in addition to their usual management skills.

# MAKE THE BUDGET WORK

THE BUDGET PROCESS in many companies has become an elaborate and time-consuming ritual that does little to drive the organization forward, and can actively prevent the development of innovative new plans.

Once the budget has been set, organizations tend to fall back on the fact that new initiatives have not been budgeted for as the excuse for not taking them up quickly or, indeed, at all.

## The idea

The leader who most clearly demonstrated that a new approach to budgeting was possible was Jack Welch, chairman and CEO of General Electric. Welch describes the typical budgeting process as either:

"The Negotiated Settlement" (in which the team presents its budget needs, management presents its financial restrictions, and it is agreed to split the difference), or "The Phoney Smile" (in which management listen politely to detailed presentations but then impose a settlement).

Welch recommends as an alternative the use of two key questions: How can we beat last year's performance? What is our competition doing, and how can we beat them?

"If you focus on these two questions, the budgeting process becomes a wide-ranging, anything-goes dialogue between the field and headquarters about opportunities and obstacles in the real world.

Through these discussions, both sides of the table jointly come up with a growth scenario that is not negotiated or imposed and cannot really be called a budget at all. It is an operating plan for the next year, filled with aspiration, primarily directional, and containing numbers that are primarily understood to be targets ..."

Another approach to creative budgeting was put in place by white goods manufacturer, Whirlpool, when they made a commitment to putting innovation at the heart of the company's strategy.

The woman charged with this initiative was Nancy Snyder: "If you're a normal organization, you do your budgeting once a year and you're locked in. So if you came up with a great idea, there'd be no money for you. What the CEO did was ask each region to set up a seed fund for innovation ... Then he said, 'I want you to fund all of the ideas that come forward. I don't want you turning down any ideas. And if you turn them down, I'm going to tell them to come to me.'"

## In practice

- The traditional budget process can lead to limited aspirations and discarded good initiatives, as managers aim for limited but acceptable growth.

- The budget could be a search for growth opportunities; an operating plan that encourages the team to hit challenging targets, with a series of "safety nets" in place.

- Budgets should be flexible enough to provide funds for good new initiatives. In an ideal world, initiatives would be encouraged at any time and seed capital would be available to develop them.

# PLAN FOR YOUR SUCCESSION

THE DECISION TO appoint your successor will normally be made by somebody else. The position may or may not go to somebody from within the organization. It is also unhealthy for leaders to attempt to ensure that their policies are continued by a like-minded new leader: change is essential and inevitable.

The best that any leader can do is to cram the organization with talented people who may have the capacity to lead the organization one day.

## The idea

John Birt, Director-General of the BBC from 1992–2000, tried hard to ensure that his strategy for the organization would continue after his tenure came to an end, and that his successor would be somebody from within the BBC who would continue to implement his management policies. He prepared a 20-year plan for the BBC and insisted on a five-month handover. His successor, chosen by the Chairman and the Board of Governors of the BBC, was an outside candidate, Greg Dyke, who had a very different leadership style.

"In my experience," wrote Dyke, "the only thing you can be certain about when dealing with long-term plans is that they will turn out to be wrong: there are too many variables for them ever to be right ... The failure of strategic plans is nobody's fault; it's just that the word changes faster, or in different directions, than predicted by the strategic planners ... John Birt wanted as his successor someone who would not disrupt what he had done so far and would carry out the first part of his 20-year plan. He wanted someone from inside the BBC who would carry the Birt-ist flame … He certainly didn't want someone like me coming in from outside who would probably never even read his plan."

Rebekah Wade, Chief Executive of Rupert Murdoch's UK's News International Ltd, was previously the editor of the media organization's *Sun* newspaper. "I always hire people who absolutely want my job. Not just in a 'that would be nice to have her job' way but with an absolute 'I can do better than her' attitude. It doesn't make for a comfortable life, but appointing really clever people, who challenge you all the time, makes a successful career."

## In practice

- Leaders can only adopt the strategies and policies that appear to be right to them during their time in office. It is a mistake to hope that your policies will continue after you have moved on.

- It is also a mistake to hope that your successor will be "someone like you". However successful you have been, every leader has a distinctive leadership style and organizations benefit from change.

- Leaders should recruit colleagues of the highest calibre, so that the organization has a good choice of internal candidates from which to choose.

- People of this calibre will make challenging colleagues, but they will help you to drive the organization to greater success.

# PART 3

# YOU AND
# THE WHOLE TEAM

# 14 ALLOW CHOICE TO DRIVE DECISIONS

LEADERS MUST SET the broad direction of an organization—the core vision—but the collective intelligence of the organization can help decide how best to achieve that vision. The more broadly this collective decision making is based, the better.

This is a form of market-driven decision: letting the market (in this case, the organization's collective talent) dictate where the organization should direct its efforts.

## The idea

Mukesh Ambani is the chairman and managing director of Reliance Industries, India's largest private sector corporation. His father, Dhirubhai Ambani, founded the company, trading in spices and then textiles, later taking the company public and diversifying into petrochemicals, telecommunications, food, power, life-sciences and other sectors.

In 2006 the company was divided into two new organizations, each headed by Dhirubhai's two sons, Mukesh and Anil. Mukesh says that he gets most satisfaction from seeing the company blazing new trails and challenging the status quo.

Reliance Industries allows its junior managers to select the areas in which they would most like to work, via a competitive process, after a six-month induction process to "teach them the Reliance way". Each Reliance business makes a presentation to the newcomers, who are then invited to choose the field in which they want to work.

"In the 1990s," says Mukesh, "finance and treasury was the in thing. Then it was marketing. In the last two years, most bright young people want to work in rural areas. This is a big mindset change ... Young people want to go to Punjab and stay there for a month to figure out what works. In telecom, when we said we would go into [rural areas], a lot of our friends thought it [was] all talk. Even the regulator was sceptical ... In retailing, they are saying, we don't want to do merchandising; we want to create those rural markets. In that sense, it is great fun. I always tell my young guys, we are going on an expedition together. When you do that, we need to support each other because we can get lost quickly ... Today it is rural areas that are making more money. I have noticed that talent is automatically motivated by larger goals and some of the brightest people want to do things that are different."

## In practice

- Leaders set the overall compass bearing but should not attempt to describe every stage of the journey.

- A well-run organization is full of intelligent people who understand the world around them. Their instincts about future trends and profitable avenues are probably correct.

- Try to create internal markets that allow colleagues to choose paths that most interest them: these paths are likely to be successful.

- Make sure that resources follow people's choices so that the organization is changed by colleagues' decisions.

## 15 BE CLEAR

---

POOR COMMUNICATION OFTEN results in a surprising lack of clarity about very important issues within an organization.

To make things more complicated, there are cultural differences in the degree of clarity that people expect or welcome.

---

## The idea

A well-led group acts in a coordinated way, following a clear plan. As business writers Mike Southon and Chris West stress: "Clarity is a much undervalued management virtue. Tell people what they are supposed to be doing and why. This may sound obvious, but surveys often reveal managers to be mired in uncertainty about what their actual job is."

To make matters worse, there are significant cultural differences as to the degree of clarity that different national groupings are used to or would welcome.

As Bryan Huang, BearingPoint Senior Vice President and China President says, "Almost all Americans or Europeans get very confused when they first visit Japan or China. Western culture places a high value on being very specific. But in Japan and China, things are more ambiguous, on purpose. This makes communication very difficult."

Huang may himself be overestimating the ease of clear communication between countries in the West: Americans have difficulty with the British tradition of understatement and self-effacement. In the Korean War, an American sector commander decided not to relieve the British 29th Brigade, who had reported their situation as being "a bit sticky". The American commander took this to mean that the situation was difficult but not disastrous; in fact, the British brigade was surrounded and about to be overrun.

Equally, it must not be assumed that all Asian countries communicate in the same way. Japanese national, Seiichi Kawasaki, Director and President of Sony (China) Ltd, draws his own distinction between the Japanese and Chinese cultures: "Japanese people are very vague. We guess at each other's meaning. But the Chinese are much more direct and clear. This open communication is much more effective."

## In practice

- Precise communication has always been difficult. The need to do business across cultural divides is making clear, two-way communication even harder and ever more important.

- All human beings are resistant, to greater or lesser degrees, to "clarity". A broad statement of intent and direction may well be generally accepted and acted on; more detailed directions may be listened to but misunderstood or ignored.

- The idea must be clear and unambiguous when first presented. Do not hedge, fudge, soften or qualify any important statement.

- Repeat your key messages many times in every possible circumstance. People need time to absorb an idea properly.

- Understand that your clear instruction will be interpreted in many different ways and that the responses that you are given may not be straightforward. Colleagues may give you the response that they think you are hoping for.

# 16 BE DEMANDING

TEAMS EXPECT leaders to be demanding. If the leader is not demanding, the team assumes that there is no urgency and that they need not put themselves out too much. A leader who is not demanding more of his or her team than they can comfortably deliver is not really leading.

## The idea

In the early days of Microsoft Corporation, Bill Gates was a famously hard taskmaster. Early employees at Microsoft Corporation worked incredibly long hours, in a chaotic but creative environment. Late-night pizzas at the office were the norm, followed by even more work into the early hours of the morning.

At the same time, the working atmosphere was extremely casual: there was no dress code; people worked the hours that they wanted to work and would sometimes take a break to see a movie, play electric guitar or set up a competitive sports session in the corridor and then get back to work.

Bill Gates himself would often sleep at the office. One programmer from these early days said, "Bill was always pushing. We'd do something I thought was really clever, and he would say, 'Why didn't you do this, or why didn't you do that two days ago?' That would get frustrating sometimes." But as another early programmer, Steve Wood, also said, "We'd often be there 24 hours a day, trying to meet a deadline or ... getting a new product out. We noticed the long hours, but it wasn't a burden. It was fun. We weren't doing it because someone was standing over us with a whip saying, 'You guys have got to do this.' We were doing it because we had stuff to do and we had to get it done."

These "Microsoft Kids" felt that they were working at the edge of a technological revolution. They were excited by their work and uncomplaining about the demands on their time, energy and creativity.

## In practice

- The leader sets the tone for the organization; if the leader is not demanding, nobody else will be.

- Being demanding is not the same as being an impossible taskmaster or an unreasonable employer. People can only work exceptionally hard on a voluntary basis and for a limited time.

- People like to be challenged at work; to feel that they are part of something important and challenging. When people are involved in this way, they will work exceptionally hard without complaint.

- Encourage this kind of environment but do not abuse people's commitment: an exceptional commitment of time and energy should be temporary.

- During these intense spells, give colleagues the opportunity to let off steam. Allow them some indulgences to reward their exceptional contribution.

- Create ways for people to have fun in the office, especially "after hours".

# BE FAIR

---

PEOPLE ARE VERY sensitive to what is "fair". This applies to what they feel is reasonable to expect from them and to what rewards they are offered. Rewards within the organization need to be consistent.

---

## The idea

Jonah Lehrer, neuroscientist and author on the psychology of decision making, describes "the ultimatum game": a key experiment into human selfishness and altruism.

One of two people ("the proposer") is given $10. He or she is then asked to make an offer of any proportion of the money to the other person ("the responder"); if the offer is accepted, both parties keep the money. It was assumed that the proposer would act selfishly and offer a minimal amount and that the responder would react rationally and take any offer as better than nothing. But, as Lehrer reports, "The researchers soon realized that their predictions were all wrong. Instead of swallowing their pride and pocketing a small profit, responders typically rejected any offer they perceived as unfair. Furthermore, proposers anticipated this angry rejection and typically tendered an offer of around five dollars. This was such a stunning result that nobody really believed it." "The fact is," says Lehrer, "that we can imagine how the other person will feel about an unfair offer. Our brains have become hard-wired to see things from the other person's perspective."

David Packard made a speech to Hewlett Packard managers in the 1960s in which he talked about the responsibilities of leaders: "Tolerance is tremendously significant. Unless you are tolerant of the people under you, you really can't do a good job of being a supervisor. You must have understanding—understanding of the little things that affect people. You must have a sense of fairness, and you must know what it is reasonable to expect of your people."

The American psychologist Frederick Herzberg's "Two factor theory" of job satisfaction suggests that people are made unhappy by what they see as bad or unfair things in their working environment, to a greater extent than they are made happy by things that are satisfactory. Preventing people from being dissatisfied is just as important as concentrating on their motivation.

John Harvey-Jones, previously chairman of ICI, confirms the importance of fairness: "Certainly my own personal experience tends to confirm Herzberg's theory that monetary reward is not in itself an incentive, but poor or unfair reward is a major disincentive … Relative rewards within the organization, unless demonstrably fairly apportioned, have the same effect."

## In practice

- People have an innate sense of what is fair. This applies to whether what they are being asked to do is "reasonable" and whether they are being treated "fairly".

- Leaders must ask people to make exceptional efforts; a key function of leadership is to assess what can reasonably be demanded.

- Rewards must be fair and be seen to be fair. An unfair reward can be disproportionately de-motivating.

- Not all rewards need to be financial, but people are equally sensitive about whether praise or other intangible rewards have been fairly allocated.

# 18 ❗ COMMUNICATE ALL OF THE TIME

It is easy for leaders to believe that they have already successfully communicated something, usually by way of a set speech, a memo, a series of emails or a plan of action discussed with senior management that should now be cascading down through the organization.

This kind of communication is hardly ever enough to embed an idea in the consciousness of the organization. To achieve this requires constant and consistent communication.

## The idea

Carly Fiorina, ex-CEO and chairman of Hewlett Packard, who oversaw the merger of Hewlett Packard with computer manufacturer Compaq, points out that change requires far more communication than might at first be imagined.

"Change, particularly systematic change of a company's entire framework, requires communication that is authentic, clear, persistent, consistent and ubiquitous. Because people hear competing messages, or resist the message, or just don't hear at all, my rule of thumb is that real change generally requires ten times the amount of communication you originally plan. And so I would use every forum, every speech, and every venue to communicate with the employees of HP. No matter who I was talking to, no matter where I was in the world, I was talking to the employees of HP."

Harvard Business School professor and writer on leadership, John

Kotter, makes the point that the communication must include all of the organization's audiences.

"Bosses, peers, staff in other parts of the organization, suppliers, government officials, or even customers ... Anyone needed to help implement the vision and strategies or anyone in a position to block implementation can be relevant."

Martha Lane Fox, co-founder of lastminute.com, says that an important element of leadership is "performance"—getting in front of people, telling them as much as you can and keeping them involved with the overall project.

"Great leadership and entrepreneurship is a lot to do with performing. I always believed that you should get as many people together, as often as possible and tell them as much as possible. Before we changed from a private company to a public company, I used to stand on a desk every Friday to speak to the team. We'd have some cakes and I'd say what happened during the week. It sent the key messages through the organization and made people feel very positive."

## In practice

- Leaders can never assume that an important communication has reached every relevant part of the organization. Communication of really important principles, ideas and directions needs constant repetition.

- In every interaction with colleagues, leaders should drive home the key messages. Interviews with the media, or presentations to external bodies, are also ways of communicating with colleagues.

- People who need to know about significant change include not only colleagues, but also the wider audience of stakeholders and potential influencers.

- Tell the team as much as you can, as often as you can. It will keep them involved, motivated and inspired.

# COMMUNICATE IN CRISIS

COMMUNICATION IS NEVER more important than when the organization is facing a crisis. There is a common tendency not to give out more information than is absolutely necessary. In fact, a lack of information will only make the situation worse.

If a leader can communicate that a particular course of action is essential and that it will be successful, people will come together to face the problem in a positive way.

## The idea

When Andrea Jung, chairman of the board and chief executive officer of Avon Products Inc, undertook a radical restructuring of the company, she relied on her belief in "hyper communication".

"I think the honesty, the speed of communicating our plans, and doing so in person—being willing to stand there instead of sending out a memo—helped enormously in that transition phase. It was interesting that so many people came up to me after I'd spoken and said: 'I have no idea if I'm still going to be here or not, but I just want you to know that it was really unique and critical that you were so honest at this point.'"

Gerard Kleisterlee, president and CEO of Dutch electronics multinational Philips, talks about the need to communicate more intensively in times of crisis: "I don't think we have to address people differently, but probably we have to communicate with them more intensively. Particularly in difficult times, in times of uncertainty ... as a leader you have to be more visible. ... If management adopts

'salami' tactics—announcing the bad news one slice at a time—
that can create a general level of uncertainty among employees ...
At this point, as the CEO, I have to be clear about the position of
the company: Is our strategy robust? [If you can] communicate that
effectively throughout the company, then a crisis can rally people. It
can awaken their fighting spirit and draw people closer together."

## In practice

- When an organization is in crisis, the rest of the organization
  needs to know about it.

- It will be impossible to hide the truth, and any attempt to play
  down the crisis will allow colleagues to feel that the situation is
  not as bad as they feared. Releasing bad news in dribs and drabs
  makes the team more anxious.

- Colleagues whose jobs may be at risk deserve to know the worst
  possible scenario as soon as possible. Keeping them informed
  and involved allows them to contribute to the solution of the
  crisis: colleagues who are stressed and badly informed will not
  be able to contribute anything at all.

- Leaders must present not simply the problem but also the
  solution: the plan of action.

- The problem and its solutions must be presented not only
  internally but also externally, to all stakeholders and to the
  media.

- Colleagues who are reassured that the organization can survive
  will be motivated to do whatever they can to help.

# COMMUNICATE SIMPLY

COMMUNICATING RELATIVELY COMPLEX ideas to a large number of people is a daunting task. The audience will listen attentively, but they will take away, at best, a few fragments of what was actually said. A leader's vision and core strategy should be reduced to a few simple and powerful statements.

## The idea

John F. Kennedy, 35th President of the United States, was elected in 1961. In his Presidential Nomination Acceptance speech, made a year earlier, he set out a bold vision of an America that could come together to solve the problems of the age, just as the pioneers of the previous century had overcome the problems of the great expansion into western territories.

"For I stand tonight facing west on what was once the last frontier. From the lands that stretch three thousand miles behind me, the pioneers of old gave up their safety, their comfort and sometimes their own lives to build a new world here in the West ... Their motto was not 'every man for himself' but 'all for the common cause'. ... Today some would say that those struggles are all over—that all the horizons have been explored—that all the battles have been won—that there is no longer an American frontier ... But I tell you the New Frontier is here, whether we seek it or not. Beyond that frontier are the uncharted areas of science and space, unsolved problems of peace and war, unconquered pockets of ignorance and prejudice, unanswered questions of poverty and surplus."

"The New Frontier" came to be a powerful phrase that encapsulated the aims of the Kennedy administration, including complex issues of labor, housing and civil rights reform.

In the same way, the very best corporate visions can be instantly grasped, at an instinctive level, by the whole organization and even by the public at large. In the 1960s, when the car rental firm Avis addressed the fact that they were second in the market to the leader, Hertz, they adopted the memorable slogan, "We try harder". The message that Avis would try harder to please customers because they were not the market leader, was instantly understood by the public and has become an iconic statement of a company's fundamental values. It was introduced by Robert Townsend, whose tenure as CEO of Avis saw the company move from loss-making to profitability, and who led the company to become a giant in the worldwide car rental market.

## In practice

- Condense your vision and key strategy into very simple statements. If you can't express them simply, they are not right.

- If you can, turn the simple statement of the core strategy into a memorable slogan. Get this right, and you will be famous.

# COMMUNICATE THE VISION

THE VISION THAT a leader has chosen for the organization is the single most important thing that must be communicated to the team. It needs to be repeated on every possible occasion, in clear and memorable terms.

## The idea

Bob Iger is the president and CEO of the Walt Disney Company and the sixth person to hold this role since the company was founded by Walt Disney in 1923. Disney's grand vision is "To make people happy". Iger sets out what he describes as his strategic vision: "To use technology to reach more people, more often, in more convenient ways".

This strategic vision led Iger to make some of Disney's most valuable properties available for streaming online; a highly controversial decision. Iger stresses the importance of putting in place the fundamental structures that will enable people to carry out the vision.

Most importantly, he emphasizes the need to communicate the vision: "One of the things that becomes very, very important for a CEO to accomplish is a strategic vision, and then to enable people by creating the right environment to carry it out. And it becomes also important to articulate that vision often because it won't get carried out unless it's both clear and well-spoken."

John Ryan, president of the Center for Creative Leadership, reminds us that it is not enough to communicate the vision to the top team: leaders must find time to communicate to the whole organization.

"The sheer time demands of serving in a leadership role can undermine our overall effectiveness as leaders. Moreover, when we do turn our attention as executives to communication, we sometimes make things even worse. In my own experience, which includes observing clients all over the world, it's clear that most organizations are very uneven in their communications. They're often good at the top. Their executive and senior management teams understand the CEO's vision and strategy. But the deeper you dive into the organization, the more muddled things get. Middle managers and frontline employees often have no idea how to connect their daily work to the larger strategy. Frequently they don't even know what the strategy is. Does that sound familiar? We shouldn't blame them for disregarding our occasional memos about 'adding value' and 'synergies' and 'thinking outside the box.' It's our fault as leaders when we don't communicate in meaningful terms that make sense throughout the entire organization."

## In practice

- A leader's vision for the organization is his or her most important contribution. Leaders must communicate that vision and create an environment that enables people to accomplish the vision.

- Communicating the vision on a few occasions at "set-piece" events will never be enough. Leaders must communicate their vision as often as possible and to as many audiences as possible, at all levels of the organization.

- The vision must be clearly presented. It must be easy to understand and it needs to appeal to achievements that people can genuinely relate to: people cannot be inspired by jargon.

# CREATE ACTION GROUPS

THE ORGANIZATION HAS many areas that need improvement, refinement or replacement. It also includes many people who need new challenges. Action groups allow colleagues to contribute their ideas and energies and to show what they are capable of.

## The idea

Allan Leighton, ex-CEO of UK's Asda supermarket chain, made great use of what he called "positive action groups".

"A great way to spot potential and keep your rising stars motivated is to introduce positive action groups, or PAGs. There are always things in an organization that need to be fixed so, if there's an issue, I put a PAG on it. They're not permanent groups: they take action quickly and then disband themselves. I choose seven or eight people with real potential from across the business. I'll pick one as leader to report directly to me, and that person may well not be the most senior man or woman in the team. However, that's part of the development process: you develop people by giving them challenging things to do."

Business authors Mike Southon and Chris West write about creating an entrepreneurial environment in larger organizations.

They recommend bringing together a collection of people with different talents to create "micro-teams" that can explore and potentially develop what they call "intrapreneurial" ideas within larger organizations, bypassing the existing business structures that tend to prevent potentially radical new ideas from emerging or from getting the support that they deserve.

They stress that new ideas must be tested "quickly, cheaply and with the minimum of fuss". The micro-team will need the necessary space, time and micro-finance; the ideal micro-team would include a relatively senior "sponsor", who can steer the project through the organization, getting it the help and support that it needs; an "innovator"—an ideas person; a "deliverer"—someone who can see the project through to completion; a sales person—someone who can demonstrate the customer demand for the new idea; and, finally, a finance person.

## In practice

- Any leader is faced with a long list of issues that need addressing which are not absolutely central to the implementation of the core vision, but still deserve attention.

- There are many talented people throughout the organization who may not have been given the opportunity to demonstrate their abilities. Form action groups of people and give them challenges.

- Put different people in charge of the groups—not necessarily the most senior—to develop people's leadership abilities.

- Create groups with the best mix of talents who are likely to reach a well-presented conclusion that will be compelling to the senior management team.

- Action groups are meant to solve real problems and may propose quite radical solutions, which should be seriously considered. Ensure that good solutions are implemented and that the action group is recognized and rewarded for its efforts by praise and recognition.

# 23 CREATE FOLLOWERS

LEADERS NEED TEAMS that will do something because it is the right thing to do for the organization, rather than because they have been told to do it.

To achieve this, leaders should avoid directing people to do specific things and, instead, try to create "followers"—people who have chosen to follow your direction.

## The idea

Anne Mulcahy of Xerox Corporation talks about the need for colleagues to "believe in a story" about the direction in which the organization is moving, so that they can embrace that direction with real commitment.

"We talk a lot about execution and the importance of it. But I actually think it's a lot more about followership—that your employees are volunteers and they can choose to wait things out if they don't believe. And that can be very damaging in a big company. So it is absolutely this essence of creating followership that becomes the most important thing that you can do as a leader ... People really have to begin to believe in a story to get passionate about the direction the company is going in ... There's nothing quite as powerful as people feeling they can have impact and make a difference. When you've got that going for you, I think it's a very powerful way to implement change."

W.L. Gore & Associates, manufacturers of the waterproof and breathable fabric Gore-tex and of many other polymer products used in a wide variety of industries, have always encouraged a work environment where employees commit to projects that they want to get involved with.

The company follows a policy where "all commitments are self-commitments". Employees must choose which projects they want to contribute to and accept the responsibilities that come with those choices. Commitments are binding, and reward is based on the contribution made to each team, so that there is both the incentive to take on more tasks and a self-regulating concern about over-commitment. An individual's contribution to a project is assessed in annual reviews by 20 peers; everyone is ranked against the rest of the business unit in terms of contribution. Gore employees have signed up for everything that they are expected to deliver.

## In practice

- Leaders need to create followers; they must present compelling reasons why people should want to follow a chosen direction.

- When colleagues have embraced a particular idea and have themselves become passionate about it and when they understand exactly what contribution they personally can make, then the organization is capable of achieving powerful change.

- People are most engaged when they have chosen the projects to which they commit themselves; personal commitment is far more powerful than enforced compliance.

- If rewards genuinely follow delivery against these commitments, the system becomes self-motivating.

# DISTANCE AND CLOSENESS

As organizational hierarchies become much flatter, and people come to expect a more human relationship with senior management, the balancing act between closeness and distance becomes much harder for the modern leader.

## The idea

Charles de Gaulle, French general and president of France, had what may now be seen as a rather old-fashioned approach to power and prestige: "There is no authority without prestige, and no prestige without distance." De Gaulle was, indeed, famous for his arrogance. He also said, "I have heard your views. They do not harmonize with mine. The decision is taken unanimously."

Rob Goffee and Gareth Jones, business authors and professors of the London School of Business, say that leaders need distance, in order to see the organization in a clear perspective, and closeness, in order to get a good grasp of what is actually going on in the business. Managing the balance between distance and closeness is a modern leadership challenge:

"Hierarchies have always been much more than structural devices. They have also been sources of meaning for people. Moving through stable hierarchies gave the illusion of becoming more of a leader. Indeed, the 'lazy' senior executive relied on the crutch of hierarchy to establish social distance, jealously guarding their status privileges as a way of establishing their difference. Those days are gone. Leaders now need distance to establish perspective, to see the big things that may shape the future of the organization, and closeness, to know what is really going on inside their business; and they cannot rely on hierarchy to supply the former. This movement between closeness and distance is rather like a dance ..."

## In practice

- Leaders need a degree of distance from the organization in order to be able to lift their heads from the detail and see the bigger picture.

- Leaders need a degree of closeness to the organization in order to get a real hands-on understanding of its processes. They also need a degree of closeness to their colleagues; people need to feel that their leader is a human being. Nobody can be genuinely inspired by a remote figure of authority.

- Too much familiarity can lead to contempt; too much distance will lead to detachment. Achieving the right balance is a key skill for the modern leader.

# DON'T GET COMPLACENT

THE POINT WILL come when all of your initial changes are in place and when everything seems to be going to plan. It is at this point that the competition will assess what you have done, be impressed for a few hours and then start working on how to take you apart. In the meantime the market—which doesn't take you personally in the way that your competitors do—will be moving inexorably on.

## The idea

Andrew Grove, founder of Intel, says it all in his much-quoted remark: "Success breeds complacency. Complacency breeds failure. Only the paranoid survive."

Another word for complacency is arrogance.

In the late 1990s, the successful British clothing retailer, Marks & Spencer, slumped suddenly and spectacularly, taking everyone by surprise. In July 2008, shares fell by 25% after the announcement of a sharp drop in sales. Profits fell from over £1 billion in 2008 to £145 million in 2001. Stuart Rose was appointed as chief executive of the company in 2004, having worked for the company previously as a young man, joining M&S as a management trainee. He says that the core values of the company—quality, service, value and innovation—had been drummed into him during his earlier years with the company, as had the company's roots: Michael Marks and Thomas Spencer had started out as market traders.

In an interview given when he first became chief executive, Rose said: "I think there is an element from what I have seen so far that people have forgotten their roots ... There has been a little bit of danger of late that we have said '[that heritage] doesn't stand for much; we are going to reinvent this business and make it something else'. It isn't. It's Marks and bloody Spencer. ... It seems to me that there is a little bit of clinging on to each other. But you can't hold hands. We live in a cruel, hard, tough commercial world. The business definitely suffered a little from the A-word—arrogance—in the mid to late-90s. It looked out of the window and found the world had passed it by."

Sir Richard Branson, chairman of Virgin Group, makes the same point. "We never let people sit on their laurels, and we keep on trying to improve things. The minute Virgin Atlantic was voted 'The airline with the best business-class seats in the world' in the UK Airline Awards, our designer was already beginning to work on the next seats in order to beat our expectations rather than our competitors. You must either stay ahead of the other people, or stay ahead of yourself, all the time. If you really put your mind to it you are normally going to find a better way. You have to keep on questioning the way people do things."

## In practice

- When companies are successful, complacency and a kind of arrogance can set in. Constant anxiety—"paranoia"—is a better frame of mind.

- Successful leaders keep the organization close to its heritage and to its customers, to ensure that they are still delivering both their original promise and the goods and services that customers currently want.

- Even at moments of great success, the organization must be looking to its next challenge, to ensure that it stays ahead.

# 26  ENCOURAGE CANDOR

In order to function as a social group, we often avoid direct communication which might lead to conflict. There is a tendency to reach for social consensus: to gloss over or ignore difficult facts and to emerge with a version of reality that is not too challenging for any member of the group.

Organizations cannot allow this human tendency to disguise the need for radical action on key issues. Colleagues must be encouraged to be frank, honest and "candid".

## The idea

The corporate leader who developed the idea of candor in business relations more than any other is Jack Welch, chairman and CEO of General Electric from 1981 to 2001.

Candor, says Welch, is all about asking hard questions. Instead of talking about how difficult the business environment is and congratulating each other on how well we have done under the circumstances, "Now imagine an environment where you take responsibility for candor. You ... would ask questions like: Isn't there a new product or service idea in this business somewhere that we just haven't thought of yet? Can we jump-start this business with an acquisition? This business is taking up so many resources. Why don't we just get the hell out of it?" Welch believes that candor brings more people into a dialogue, which creates an "idea rich" environment. It also speeds things up: "When ideas are in everyone's face, they can be debated rapidly, expanded and enhanced, and acted upon."

Although many corporations have accepted this "in your face" way of conducting business, some national cultures (and many people within any culture) are resistant to the approach, and leaders should bear this in mind.

Jun Tang, president of Microsoft China, highlights the fact that managers may cause offence by speaking too bluntly and causing "loss of face".

"One can hurt someone's feelings forever. American culture is very direct. But [Chinese] people are so sensitive. Sensitivity is part of their 5,000-year-old culture." The problem is not only about managers causing offence to members of the team: employees who bring a problem to the attention of a manager could be seen as implying a criticism of that manager, a suggestion that the manager is in some way responsible.

## In practice

- Organizations cannot function successfully with the kind of "social niceties" that are common in everyday life; problems must be addressed frankly and honestly.

- Honest and candid discussions about business issues get to the heart of a problem, reveal stark but realistic choices and speed up business responses. Candor also opens up useful debate by inviting real dialogue about issues.

- In some cultures, and for some people in all cultures, there is real resistance to this kind of candid behavior, which implies criticism and blame.

- The invitation to colleagues to behave with real "candor" must be carefully presented, along with reassurances that frank-speaking will not be misconstrued or penalized. Cultural differences must be taken into account.

# ENCOURAGE
# REAL DEBATE

EVERYONE WANTS TO please the boss, who runs the risk that he or she will be the last person to know that the organization has a problem.

## The idea

Dieter Zetsche, chairman of Daimler AG and head of Mercedes Benz Cars, says: "The higher you climb up the ladder, the more people will tell you what a great guy you are. The worst trap you can fall into is believing them. It's important to encourage people to give you feedback and to disagree if they have a different opinion. It depends on your reaction. Otherwise you are totally alone. You will lose touch and ultimately make decisions which are really dumb."

Alan Mulally, president and CEO of Ford Motor Company, introduced a weekly leadership meeting at which every department was represented in order to review key indicators for each project, which were represented by "stop light" color codes: red, orange or green, to represent the project's status. "I remember the first couple of weeks, we got the process going, everybody was kind of getting familiar with it, and it seemed like it was OK. And then all the stop light charts started to get filled in and everything was green, and I stopped the meeting and I said, 'Fellas and ladies, we just lost $12 billion! And everything is green? Aren't there just a few things that need special attention?' And in the next week ... because you've got to make it safe because the minute that you're intimidating, the minute that it's not comfortable to show you how it is, everything will be green, right? So the next week, boom. Up comes a bright red." Mulally applauded the red light and asked the project manager what he needed to fix the problem. A launch was behind schedule; more technical and manufacturing support was needed to get the vehicles out on time. The team discussed the issues and volunteered their departments' assistance. Three weeks later the project was on "orange" and in another two weeks it was "green".

After this experience, the team members were more prepared to be honest in their assessments and to flag up issues.

## In practice

- People tend to present leaders with good news and will tend to put the best gloss on the situation rather than to flag up a genuine problem.

- Only when problems have been acknowledged can help be supplied and a solution found. Teams must be encouraged to recognize real problems honestly and to debate them frankly.

- Leaders can block this process by reacting negatively to bad news and by shouting at the messenger.

- Open and non-judgemental debate must be encouraged to bring problems into the open so that the team can find a solution.

# **ENGAGE PEOPLE'S EMOTIONS**

A LEADER'S VISION must connect with people at an emotional level if it is to change their behavior.

## The idea

Robert McKee is a successful screenwriter, lecturer and author who believes that leaders need to use the art of storytelling to engage the team at an emotional level.

"A big part of a CEO's job is to motivate people to reach certain goals. To do that, he or she must engage their emotions, and the key to their hearts is story. There are two ways to persuade people. The first is by using conventional rhetoric, which is what most executives are trained in. It's an intellectual process, and in the business world it usually consists of a PowerPoint slide presentation in which you say, 'Here is our company's biggest challenge, and here is what we need to do to prosper'. And you build your case by giving statistics and facts and quotes from authorities. But there are two problems with rhetoric. First, the people you're talking to have their own set of authorities, statistics, and experiences. While you're trying to persuade them, they are arguing with you in their heads. Second, if you do succeed in persuading them, you've done so only on an intellectual basis. That's not good enough, because people are not inspired to act by reason alone. The other way to persuade people— and ultimately a much more powerful way—is by uniting an idea with an emotion. The best way to do that is by telling a compelling story. In a story, you not only weave a lot of information into the telling but you also arouse your listener's emotions and energy."

Storytelling, says McKee, expresses how and why life changes. Stories "display the struggle between expectation and reality in all its nastiness".

When Greg Dyke, previous Director General of the BBC, set about instigating a programme of culture change called *Making it Happen*, his vision was to make the BBC "the most creative organization in the world".

He commissioned a series of short films that celebrated the achievements of the BBC's unsung heroes. "These films, and dozens of others like them, opened the eyes of BBC people to the scale and range of the organization and made them proud of what was being achieved and of those involved. The real point about *Making it Happen* was that it engaged people's emotions, not just their brains. Cultural change is above all an emotional experience, not an intellectual one."

# In practice

- People can be convinced by a compelling argument, but this may not change their behavior. To motivate and inspire people, a leader needs to engage their emotions.

- We all tend to remember and understand events as a series of stories; this is how we try to make sense of what we experience.

- In compelling stories, something that is desired is thwarted by antagonistic forces that must be overcome.

- A leader's vision—the struggle that the organization faces to achieve its goal—can be framed as a compelling story.

# GET FEEDBACK

LEADERS CANNOT MAKE well-informed decisions unless they know what is really happening in an organization. Getting out of the office and meeting people face to face is the best way to achieve this.

## The idea

Anne Mulcahy, chairman and former CEO of Xerox Corporation, says that she relies on getting "up close and personal".

"I stay in touch by staying in touch. You've got to be out there. You've got to be visiting your operations. You've got to be doing town meetings. You've got to be doing round-tables. There are plenty of avenues for getting feedback, but there's nothing that substitutes for the dialogue that you can have with people on the ground, with your customers in terms of how they view the company. I think it is really powerful, and it's something that I expect our entire management team to do, as well. This is not an arm's-length exercise. You've got to get up close and personal. You've got to give people permission to give you tough news, not shoot the messenger, thank people for identifying problems early and giving you the opportunity to solve them. So I think part of it is the way you handle candid feedback, but the other part is being present. Nothing replaces sitting around a table and really asking people what's working, what's not working, what's getting in their way, how do we help? I do a lot of that and I think it is the most important thing I do."

Archie Norman, former chief executive and chairman of UK grocery chain Asda, says that when organizations are in difficulty, it is essential to meet people "on the front line":

"In problematic companies, the leader can't rely on the information that is easily and readily available. You've got to go to the front line, the people who are dealing with the customers, and get them to say the things they would never have said to the preceding management or chief executive. Great leaders rarely respect the protocols of hierarchy. Having a drink with a warehouse manager can tell you more about what's going on than all the spreadsheets in the finance department combined."

## In practice

- Leaders need accurate feedback about the organization before they can make decisions about change.

- Set-piece "town meetings" or similar structured events are a good way of establishing a feedback process. People need proof that they are being listened to and that their comments are being acted on.

- The most effective way to get real feedback is to get out of the office and talk to colleagues and customers in one-to-one meetings and small round-table sessions.

- Don't pass judgement on what people tell you. Thank them for their views and for giving you the opportunity to address the issues revealed.

# 30 GET PEOPLE ALIGNED

THE TEAM MUST not only understand the vision, they must make a personal commitment to it and feel excited and rewarded as the organization makes steps towards achieving the vision.

This is a question of leadership and inspiration rather than of management and organization—change then begins to emerge naturally and organically, without having to be driven from the centre.

## The idea

Harvard Business School professor John Kotter uses the term "alignment" to define the process. "To an audience that has been over-educated on management and under-educated in leadership, the idea of getting people moving in the same direction appears to be an organizational problem. It is not. Organizing is a managerial process with a different function and character. The relevant activity here is called aligning."

Kotter's definition of alignment is "communicating the direction to those whose cooperation may be needed so as to create coalitions that understand the vision and that are committed to its achievement".

Two other Harvard Business School professors, Michael Beer and Nitin Nohria, developed a theory to describe the two very different approaches to change that they had observed in modern organizations. They defined these as "Theory E and Theory O" of change. They use words such as "involvement" and "commitment" to describe what Kotter calls "alignment". They stress that when people have become involved in this way, they are able to learn from experience and to adapt their behavior of their own accord to keep the vision on track:

"Theory E has as its purpose the creation of economic value, often expressed as shareholder value. Its focus is on formal structure and systems. It is driven from the top with extensive help from consultants and financial incentives. Change is planned and programmatic. Theory O has as its purpose the development of the organization's human capability to implement strategy and to learn from actions taken about the effectiveness of changes made. Its focus is on the development of a high-commitment culture. Its means consist of high involvement, and consultants and incentives are relied on far less to drive change. Change is emergent, less planned and programmatic."

## In practice

- Organizations can only achieve their goals when the team members have committed themselves at a personal level. This may come from the intangible rewards of shared endeavor as much as from more obvious self-interest.

- This level of commitment can only be achieved by a process of unremitting communication. Some colleagues will attempt to "sit out" the change process for long enough for senior management to lose interest.

- When people have taken the programme to heart, they will learn from experience and adapt, having the end goal firmly in their sights.

- This approach to change is emergent and organic, rather than being driven from the top down.

# GIVE PEOPLE AUTONOMY

SUCCESSFUL LEADERS OFFER substantial autonomy to members of the team and to parts of the business. Individuals are empowered and respond to this; decision making is de-centralized, bringing more opinion and experience into the process; whole units can be allowed to take control of their own destiny while remaining "part of the family".

## The idea

Harsh Mariwala, chairman and MD of Indian health and beauty group Marico Ltd, promotes a culture of autonomy and argues that decision making should always be decentralized, with leaders contributing only where they can "add value".

"My trust level in people is very high. For example, in my company, my colleagues can make their own decisions, including in financial matters. I have never regretted this culture ... I don't make any day-to-day decisions. It is all left to my team. In that sense, leadership should be based on decentralized decision making. Leaders should be involved only if they add value to any decision, not otherwise."

William Weldon, Chief Executive Officer of Johnson & Johnson, thinks that his company is "the reference company for being decentralized" in the way that it delegates responsibility for local markets to local teams.

"The men and women who run our businesses around the world usually are people who grew up in those markets, understand those markets and develop themselves in those markets. They can relate to the needs of the customer, whoever that customer may be ... the problem with centralization is if one person makes one mistake, it can cripple the whole organization. This way, you've got wonderful people running businesses. You have to have confidence in them, but you let them run it—and you don't have to worry about making that one big mistake."

Reynold Levy, president of the Lincoln Center for the Performing Arts in New York City, says: "Our growth has been organic growth. You know, the Chamber Music Society of Lincoln Center, the Film Society of Lincoln Center, Jazz at Lincoln Center were originally concerts produced by Lincoln Center and then they found their own audience and their own support and they became their own institutions. So, our approach has not been to acquire arts institutions but to grow them naturally ... One of the functions of the organization I run is to find new audiences for different art forms, create institutions and then spin them off. They remain part of the family, but they have their own independence and autonomy."

## In practice

- Trust colleagues and give them as much scope for independent action as possible.

- Decentralize decision making so that many opinions and wide experience influence the organization's decisions. This reduces risk.

- Move decision making closer to the consumer. Intervene only when you are certain that you have a unique contribution to make.

- Consider giving a high degree of autonomy to devolved operations; give them overall objectives and allow them to deliver results within these parameters.

# GIVE THE TEAM THE TOOLS TO DO THE JOB

ONE OF THE most important functions of leadership is to ensure that the team has the tools to do the job. This is a very wide-ranging responsibility that includes not only ensuring that the team has the most efficient and up-to-date kit that they need to function effectively, but also that team members are kept informed about the most recent developments in the organization.

## The idea

Fred Smith, founder, chairman, president and CEO of FedEx, believes that one of the main functions of the company's top management is to support the "frontline folks" by enabling them to deliver FedEx's "purple promise": a deceptively simple-sounding vision: "To make every customer experience outstanding".

Advances in technology have allowed the company to give more control to these frontline folks, and the company's management see their main function as keeping their team as well-equipped as possible.

"I mean, the power that we are putting in the hands of our pick-up and delivery people, in our airplanes and our trucks and our sortation equipment; it's fantastic compared to what was possible just a few years ago ... The most important element in the FedEx system are the people that are out there, the frontline folks that are delivering what we call our 'purple promise', and the frontline management equally so. So we've always looked at it that the top management of the organization's job is to try to make their job easy

... give them the best tools, give them the best service, give them the best methodology."

Business and management consultant and writer Marshall Goldsmith reminds us that there are important ways in which we can fail to give teams the tools to do the job: "withholding information" is a good example. Withholding information, says Goldsmith, is often unintentional but it is nevertheless effectively a power-play, and one that has a pernicious effect. "We do this when we are too busy to get back to someone with valuable information. We do this when we forget to include someone in our discussions or meetings. We do this when we delegate a task to our subordinates but don't take the time to show them exactly how we want the task done."

## In practice

- Ensuring that the team has the right tools to do the job includes physical kit, back-up, efficient methodologies and operating systems.

- Having confidence that the management team is well-equipped to deal with any new problems that may arise, and that there is a system in place to deal with these, is another form of back-up for the team.

- Some things that leaders do—even unintentionally—prevent the team from having everything they need to do the job. Withholding information is a good example.

# 33  INVOLVE THE TEAM

A TEAM THAT has fully understood the vision and the broad strategy can be trusted to make the right decisions on its own initiative. Such a team is also a hugely effective support system that will "take care of business" in difficult times.

## The idea

The British Admiral, Horatio Nelson, victor of the Battle of Trafalgar, is one of Britain's national heroes. By destroying the navies of France and their allies at Trafalgar during the war with revolutionary France, Nelson ensured that Britain would not face invasion from France, across the English Channel. It is Nelson who popularized the idea of a fighting team as a "band of brothers".

Quoting from Shakespeare, Nelson had written earlier in his career about the captains under his command. "Such a gallant set of fellows! Such a band of brothers! My heart swells at the thought of them!"

It was Nelson who forged this team, entertaining the captains in his fleet for informal suppers on board his flag ship; discussing the overall war situation, his strategy and preferred tactics.

As a result, in the smoke and confusion of battle, the band of brothers could be trusted to act on their own initiative, to use the tactics most likely to bring victory, and to have the overall strategic picture constantly in mind.

India's Reliance Industries was founded by Dhirubhai Ambani. His son, Mukesh, recounts the difficulties that the company faced when his father's cousin, a senior company executive, died, soon after which Dhirubhai suffered a stroke.

Mukesh stresses that because he had involved his colleagues in an "open system" of management, there was strength in depth across the organization to cope with the death of a senior executive and the temporary incapacity of the founder.

"That was a huge blow ... two major events in five months. From three of us running the business, for some time, I suddenly became alone ... This is where investing in talent works ... there was no sense of panic. The whole picture was in my head. That was the strength of the open system. If I had kept everything close to my chest, it would have been difficult. We had excellent people across the company ... there was a plan in place. We just kept our heads down and executed it."

## In practice

- People can only make a real commitment to an organization's goals when they have been consulted and involved in the process and have committed themselves on a personal level.

- When leaders are open with their teams and involve them in the goal-setting and planning process, the team becomes self-motivating and self-sufficient.

- People who fully understand the organization's goals can be trusted to act on their own initiative; this speeds up decisions and lets the person closest to the action make key tactical decisions.

- An involved team can function successfully for extended periods without input from senior management.

# 34

## MAKE IT FUN

THERE IS EVERY reason to try to create an atmosphere at work in which people have fun. In ventures that depend on creative talent, a working environment that encourages play brings people together, breaks down barriers and creates an atmosphere of easygoing, collaborative endeavor.

In other environments, laughter can be the essential social lubricant that reduces stress levels and keeps teams of people working together on difficult projects.

## The idea

Dan Nye, CEO of the business social networking site LinkedIn from 2007 to 2009, explains how the rapidly growing company went out of its way to create an atmosphere where talented young people could come together, have fun—and work late.

"We have a big game room where there's a PlayStation 2 and the game *Guitar Hero* ... We've also got a ping pong table and a pool table. What's the idea behind all the games? It gets people from across functions interacting, communicating and playing. We're trying to build social bonds and break down barriers between groups. We also do it so people can grab something to eat or play a quick game and keep working late. It's a great business decision."

Jacqueline Novogratz is a venture philanthropist with Acumen Fund, a non-profit venture that sets out to tackle global poverty. She leads entrepreneurial local projects around the world, many of which are run by women. She talks about the importance of shared laughter and about the fact that, at the most basic level, dignity is a more important driver than money.

"The real lesson for me was how that dignity is so much more important to the human spirit than wealth. And that what these women, as all of us, needed was to know that we could cover basic needs, but to have the power of being able to say no to things that we didn't want, that we didn't want to do. And so leadership as a way of inspiring, listening, and letting people, you know, grow themselves in their own way. And it was a small experience in some ways, and yet one that I think about all the time that taught me so much about listening and dignity—and laughter as a really, really key component. The more stressed I got, the less anything worked; and the more we could laugh, the more we got done."

## In practice

- If you want people to enjoy themselves at work, try to make work a more fun place to be.

- Having fun at work breaks down barriers and creates informal groups that cross established hierarchies.

- When there is fun at work, people are less keen to leave.

- In difficult human enterprises, shared laughter can be the vital element that keeps the endeavor alive.

# OPTIONS AND CONSENSUS

CHANGE IS IMPLEMENTED more quickly and successfully when alternative options have been discussed in advance, and when the team as a whole has reached a consensus decision as to the right way forward.

A team that has been through this process will work smoothly towards the objective, understanding the various issues and alternatives.

## The idea

Sir John Harvey-Jones, ex-chairman of chemicals company ICI from 1982 to 1987, worked closely with Japanese organizations and saw the benefits of their more consensual approach to decision-taking.

"Those of us who have worked with the Japanese and who admire their business achievements, as I do, know how long it takes the Japanese to reach a decision. One is lulled into a totally false sense of security by the apparently endless debate and the thoroughness of the involvement of people at every level of the organization in the decision, because when the action stage comes, they move like greased lightning."

ICI licensed a chemical plant to a Japanese manufacturer and loaned them an ICI engineer as part of the deal. ICI began to build a UK plant at the same time that the Japanese company began work on their identical plant in Japan. "After four months we were already breaking ground and priding ourselves on being ahead of the Far Eastern opposition who, according to our engineer, were still endlessly debating items of the design and equipment. Imagine our chagrin when not only did they complete their plant seven months before us, but it also worked at first go while ours suffered the usual teething troubles and only achieved its flowsheet some three months after start-up."

This principle of consensus-seeking is featured in *The Toyota Way*: a set of principles set out by the Toyota Motor Corporation in 2001 to describe the system of values that should underpin every aspect of corporate behavior. Principle 13 talks about consensus:

"Make decisions slowly by consensus, thoroughly considering all options; implement decisions rapidly (*nemawashi*). Do not pick a single direction and go down that one path until you have thoroughly considered alternatives. When you have picked, move quickly and continuously down the path. *Nemawashi* is the process of discussing problems and potential solutions with all of those affected, to collect their ideas and get agreement on a path forward. This consensus process, though time-consuming, helps broaden the search for solutions, and once a decision is made, the stage is set for rapid implementation."

## In practice

* Leaders tend to believe that their role is to consider the options, take the advice of colleagues and experts, and then personally to make a decision.

* In a consultative process that involves the wider team, issues are debated by large sections of the organization. Problems, consequences and wider issues are more likely to be explored in depth.

* Once the organization has reached a consensus decision, the thorough understanding of the process by the team as a whole,

and the prediction and avoidance of likely difficulties, greatly speeds up the process of implementation.

# 36 TRANSFORM THE TEAM

EFFECTIVE LEADERS DO not direct the team from "outside". They join the team and motivate people by establishing goals and directions with which people genuinely identify. The purpose of the organization becomes a common purpose, and people start to take ownership of their work.

## The idea

Leadership authority James MacGregor Burns introduced the concept of Transformational Leadership. He contrasts this with Transactional Leadership, in which leaders essentially "do a deal" with the people they lead, exchanging one thing of value for another—giving people money for their labor being the obvious example of such a transaction.

Transformational Leadership is different. This happens, Burns argues, when "one or more persons engage with others in such a way that leaders and followers raise one another to higher levels of motivation". This kind of leadership is a "transformation" not an "exchange". It is a mutual process in which leaders and followers are all part of the same endeavor; people encourage and support each other; they engage with the purpose of the organization and take ownership of their work. Transformational leaders must lead by example; they will need to earn their colleagues' trust, admiration, loyalty and respect.

Jarvis Snook, CEO of UK building group Rok, recalls his experience as a works manager with a local building firm earlier in his career. He talks about the workforce: "They were paid the minimum the industry could get away with, and no one asked them their view or opinion. Their main reason for coming in to work was to have a chat with their mates. I talked to them about customer service—'If Mrs Jones wants her back bedroom decorated in time for Christmas, then stay on an hour extra in the evening and we'll pay you the overtime.' The company hadn't done that before; it was steeped in process—the workforce was just a tool." Performance improved and Snook was appointed to the board of the company. "It took me a while to work out what I'd done, but I'd changed the workers' perception of themselves; they became a valued part of the company, not a tool. They were more energized about what they were delivering for the business."

## In practice

- Effective leaders work as part of the team. They motivate and inspire people as part of a group effort.

- Transformational Leadership requires impressive personal characteristics; the successful leader will need to earn people's trust, admiration, loyalty and respect.

- Successful transformation begins to support itself; colleagues encourage each other; leaders are themselves motivated and supported by their teams.

- People take ownership of their work and are personally rewarded by the organization's success.

# TRUST YOUR EMPLOYEES

An organization that does not trust its employees creates an atmosphere of mistrust. People respond well to being trusted, and tend to behave badly when they are not.

## The idea

Bhaskar Bhat, managing director of Titan Industries Ltd, the Indian watch manufacturer, believes that well-motivated colleagues who are empowered to make sensible choices can be trusted to make decisions that are in the best interest of the organization.

"I truly believe that given the right motivation, people will naturally choose their level of responsibility and do their task to the fullest satisfaction of the organization, without supervision. You don't need to tell a guy to travel second class for cutting costs if you tell him at the same time that he can fly if there is a personal emergency like his mother being sick. He will do it willingly. Then you don't need a board or top management team to supervise."

David Packard and Bill Hewlett, founders of Hewlett-Packard Company, are famous for their philosophy of placing trust in their workforce.

Early in his career, Packard had worked for General Electric (GE). "GE was especially zealous about guarding its tool and parts bins to make sure employees didn't steal anything. Faced with this obvious display of distrust, many employees set out to prove it justified, walking off with tools or parts whenever they could." The irony was that most of GE employees were using these tools or parts in job-related or skill-enhancing projects.

When Hewlett-Packard was a young company, the founders decided that part bins and storerooms in their plants would always be open. "Coming into the plant one weekend to do some work, Bill Hewlett stopped off at a company storeroom to pick up a microscope. Finding the equipment cage locked, he broke open the latch and left a note insisting that the room not be locked again."

Packard argues that access to tools and parts helped people who wanted to work on new ideas at home or weekends and were also a symbol of trust: "a trust that is central to the way HP does business".

## In practice

- Colleagues within organizations that are well led and aligned to a common purpose can be trusted.

- If a leader cannot trust the people in the organization, then something has gone badly wrong and must be fixed. The occasional abuse of trust is an aberration that must be dealt with and then forgotten.

- An atmosphere of mistrust encourages people to behave badly.

- Colleagues are often willing and eager to use their own time for the good of the organization. An atmosphere of trust encourages and enables this.

## 38 WALK AROUND

LEADERS CAN EASILY become isolated from grass-roots issues. "Management by walking around" is a very effective way of ensuring that you understand the organization from the bottom up.

## The idea

Gregg Steinhafel, chairman and CEO of USA retailer Target Organization, spends a lot of time "walking stores".

"I think it's important that leaders ... don't become isolated. You have to go to the source; you have to spend a lot of time in your stores and a lot of time in your competitors' stores ... I come in and I want to see how does the store feel? Is it clean? Are the brand standards right? I quickly look at the check lane, is there anybody waiting in line? And I walk the store to see, is this a compelling environment? Am I excited to be here? Are there fun things on the end caps? Do I believe that there is a great value and an engaged team that comes up and greets me and says, 'Can I help you find something?' So I look for what I would expect our guests would want to have in a Target store experience and that's how I walk a store."

John Kotter, business author and professor at Harvard Business School, recalls a conversation that he had while consulting for Dow Jones & Company, the American financial information company.

A Dow-Jones executive said, "We don't let the organizational structure constrain us. We always go right to the individual who has information we need. This puts us in contact with a lot of lower-level and more junior employees, and gives us a first-hand feeling for who they are and what they are good at."

# In practice

- There is no replacement for visiting the front line—the place where the organization meets its customers.

- Leaders can easily become isolated from colleagues who are working at the front line. These colleagues know what the problems are, and will demonstrate whether what the leadership wants to happen has actually been successfully communicated.

- Quality in delivery requires huge attention to detail throughout the organization.

- The hierarchy of the organization gets in the way of direct communication: talking directly to the people who are most likely to understand the problem has the additional benefit of introducing you to talented people throughout the organization.

# 39 WORK WITH THE TEAM YOU HAVE

AT SOME POINT in their career, most leaders will take over an existing operation and its team. If the operation has been under-performing, there is a temptation to start afresh; to bring in a new team to solve the problem.

## The idea

Louis Gerstner, who brought about a remarkable turnaround of the failing computer giant, IBM, in the 1990s, confirms that he decided that it would be wrong to attempt to bring in a new team from outside.

"I think it would have been absolutely naïve—as well as dangerous—if I had come into a company as complex as IBM with a plan to impose a band of outsiders to somehow magically run the place better than the people who were there in the first place. I've entered many companies from the outside, and based on my experience, you might be able to pull that off in a relatively simple industry and under optimal conditions. It certainly wasn't going to work at IBM. It was too big and too complex a structure. More importantly, the company was brimming with talented people, who had unique experience. If I didn't give players on the home team a chance, they'd simply take their talent and knowledge and go somewhere else. I just had to find the teammates who were ready to try to do things in a different way."

Robert Mondavi, founder of California's Robert Mondavi Winery, argues that it is best to work with people as they are. "Understand that you cannot change people. You might improve them, but you can't change anyone but yourself. Accept people the way they are. Accept their differences and work with them the way they are. I learned this after about 70 years of life, and it is amazing what peace of mind I found when I finally understood it."

## In practice

- If a leader takes over a failing operation, it is deeply unlikely that the existing team are collectively responsible for the failure. That failure is the responsibility of the previous leadership.

- A new team will not be able to grasp the detail of a large and complex organization quickly enough.

- The talent of the existing team will be lost to the competition if the new leadership fails to engage that talent and to make it part of the recovery plan.

- Anybody who understands the need for a new approach can be part of the recovery.

- Work with people as you find them.

# PART 4
# YOU AND THE ORGANIZATION

# 40 | BE DIPLOMATIC

THERE ARE MANY aspects of a leader's role that demand diplomacy. A key role is to facilitate dialogue between people with varied talents, who may not naturally agree on the way forward.

Leaders spend much of their time focusing on winning; on out-performing the market or surprising the competition. This requires a combative frame of mind.

With all stakeholders, and especially with colleagues, leaders must facilitate, not confront.

## The idea

There are many different facets to diplomacy, but the essential task is to encourage creativity, real contribution and independence of thinking in colleagues while keeping them aligned with the chosen direction.

Sound ideas must not be belittled because they have already been thought of; people with excellent ideas that do not fit the current vision must be thanked and let down gently; the team must be encouraged to have genuinely radical and new ideas.

Bill Hewlett, co-founder of Hewlett Packard, was often praised for his method of dealing with engineers whose creative ideas were the lifeblood of the company. This was described as Bill's "hat-wearing process".

"On first being approached by a creative inventor with unbridled enthusiasm for a new idea, Bill immediately put on a hat called 'enthusiasm'. He would listen, express excitement where appropriate and appreciation in general, while asking a few rather general and not too pointed questions. A few days later, he would get back to the inventor wearing a hat called 'inquisition'. This was the time for very pointed questions, a thorough probing of the idea, lots of give-and-take. Without final decision, the session was adjourned. Shortly thereafter, Bill would put on his 'decision' hat and meet once again with the inventor. With appropriate logic and sensitivity, judgement was rendered and a decision made about the idea. This process provided the inventor with a sense of satisfaction, even when the decision went against the project—a vitally important outcome for engendering continued enthusiasm and creativity."

Leadership development consultant and author, Marshall Goldsmith, cautions against being unable to stop oneself from commenting on a colleague's sound idea.

"It is extremely difficult for successful people to listen to other people tell them something that they already know without communicating somehow that (a) we already knew that and (b) we know a better way." The problem is that this takes away the ownership of the idea and dramatically reduces the colleague's commitment to it. The successful diplomat will channel that colleague's enthusiasm and not deprecate it.

## In practice

- Many excellent and even brilliant ideas do not fit the overall vision. Welcome the idea; find time to discuss it in detail; explain carefully later why it cannot be used at the moment and thank the contributor.

- When colleagues have a sound idea that has already been thought through and is part of the overall vision, do not belittle this by "adding value". Welcome the idea and let the colleague keep ownership of it.

- Diplomacy is needed in dealing not only with the executive team, but also with all of the organization's stakeholders: employees, shareholders, suppliers, the media.

# 41 BE MERITOCRATIC

IT IS ESSENTIAL to recognize and reward people on the basis of their merit.

Nothing demotivates colleagues more effectively than the belief that other people are being rewarded for reasons that have nothing to do with talent, effort and results.

A true meritocracy also demands that people who produce exceptional results are rewarded more highly than other people and that the brightest and the best are identified as future managers and leaders.

## The idea

The first and fundamental aspect of a meritocracy is even-handedness. Walter Wriston, former CEO of Citicorp, describes the motivating force of being seen to operate in a meritocratic way.

"People like to be on a winning team. If they think that [management] know what they are doing and treat their people with respect, and that they are running a meritocracy, people will be motivated. We always made it clear that we didn't care about family status, or the color of your passport, or your race or gender; all we cared about was if you could do the job. I think that has a tremendous motivating force."

Anne Mulcahy, chairman and former chief executive officer of Xerox Corporation, was formerly the company's vice president of human resources. This taught her the importance of candid assessment and persuaded her that people normally get very little honest feedback from their companies.

"It became very much a mantra for me, to [create] a culture that assessed people accurately and really dealt with people fairly. The other piece is the importance of talent development. Not everybody is created equal, and it's important for companies to identify those high potentials and treat them differently, accelerate their development and pay them more. That process is so incredibly important to developing first-class leadership in a company. I think sometimes companies get confused with egalitarian processes that they think are the fairest, and that is not what companies need. Companies need to be very selective about identifying talent and investing in those leaders of the future."

When Carly Fiorina took over as CEO of Hewlett Packard in 1999, she also felt the need to put in place a rigorous system of differentiation.

"We would move away from the peanut butter approach of spreading ratings and merit pay evenly across the organization. Managers were expected to evaluate employee performance honestly and stand behind their decisions. Step by step we would learn to become, once again, a meritocracy."

## In practice

- Colleagues must be treated even-handedly. People must be selected and rewarded on the basis of their talents and abilities only.

- In a meritocracy, harder work and exceptional efforts are rewarded above the average. Spreading reward evenly is not meritocratic.

- The most talented must be identified as potential managers and leaders of the futures.

- It must be open to anybody in the organization to be able to join this team of potential leaders.

# CREATE AN ENTREPRENEURIAL CULTURE

Studies show that successful entrepreneurs do not have better ideas than other people: they have more ideas, and work harder to try to turn them into reality. They have many failures, but occasional big successes.

## The idea

William Weldon, CEO of pharmaceutical giant Johnson & Johnson, talks about the way in which his organization encourages groups of people to form mini business units to explore new product areas.

"We have what we call internal ventures ... who may put forward a recommendation for something that can be done ... So they put together a business plan, present it, put together a budget with it and then we allow that group to go off and work on that. We create other environments ... where we may bring people from the consumer, pharmaceutical and medical device and diagnostics groups together to share what they are doing. And, out of that, they will generate ideas where they can work together to bring products forward. It's usually better when they generate them rather than when we try and impose upon them."

Carol Bartz, CEO of Yahoo! and previously head of Autodesk, Inc, says, "I think the best way is for a CEO to create a culture that allows people to experiment and fail and not be ostracized for that. Innovation comes from experimentation; it comes from ideas, it comes from trying things and it comes from taking risks. You need a culture and environment that says taking risks is not only acceptable, but is rewarding. A few years back, when I was CEO of Autodesk, I had a saying: 'Fail, fast forward'. What it meant was, try something and if you fail, figure it out as fast as you can and move forward. Rather than be afraid to try anything because you might be wrong."

The inventor, James Dyson, works hard at encouraging new ideas. "Getting rid of that cynicism about new ideas is terribly important if a company is to succeed. When someone has a good idea I say, 'That's great'. I don't reject it; I look at it. It is about praising people who have good ideas and protecting them because ideas are fragile things."

## In practice

- An organization that is not constantly producing innovative ideas will quickly be overtaken by the competition.

- The organization itself is the best source of ideas about productive and profitable innovation. Try to create an entrepreneurial atmosphere throughout the organization.

- Teams can be brought together temporarily to work up and present new ideas. Bring together people from different disciplines with a wide variety of skills. Keep initial costs low.

- The majority of ideas will not be taken forward. Reassure colleagues that this is normal and inevitable. People must gain recognition for trying. Never criticize a team for "failing"—they have explored a good idea; it didn't work out.

- Give the few successes a lot of recognition, to encourage the teams working on other projects.

- Encourage teams to generate their own new ideas to explore. Never criticize or run down a new idea.

# 43 CUT DOWN ON MEETINGS

LEADERS IN MOST modern organizations will find themselves pressured to attend a large number of meetings. Attendees feel that they have the leader's attention and a direct route to executive action if needed. Too many meetings eat into a leader's available time, distracting from core issues.

## The idea

John and Forrest Mars, sons of Forrest Mars Sr., ran Mars Inc as a fairly stripped-down operation. Salaries were high in comparison with competitor companies, but conditions were egalitarian. Everyone flew economy and did their own photocopying. There were no executive bathrooms or reserved parking places. Meetings were as infrequent, short and efficient as possible.

Alan Leighton, ex-CEO of Asda, spent time early in his career at Mars UK, and took this "meetings averse" culture with him. Internal meetings at Asda were often conducted with attendees standing, to encourage people to be brief. Leighton argues for keeping the number of meetings attended by the leader to a minimum.

"Not spending time in back-to-back meetings leaves more time for productive work, such as looking after the customer and listening to the operators. The trick is to make the few meetings you do agree to attend really effective. I'm very aware that I'm constantly under time pressure. It's important for me only to do the things that really matter and to spend my time on important issues. If I don't manage my time effectively, I won't run the organization well, and I'll then become exhausted and demoralized. I don't need unnecessary meetings."

Meeting key clients and customers face to face is still a good use of a leader's time, which can involve considerable amounts of time travelling. Don Birch, managing partner of China Opportunities Ltd, talks about the future of virtual meetings.

"While there is no substitute for meeting the customer or colleague face to face, both the price and the functionality of remote meetings have improved significantly in the past few years. High-end services provide uncanny 'same room' presence and numerous low-cost Internet services make it easy and simple to conference-call across the world, interfacing voice, video, interactive presentations and text. While it is true that [people] prefer physical presence, the facilitation of Smart Meetings will mean that at least some of the journeys will be in cyber-space rather than in the back of a plane."

## In practice

- Be ruthless about which meetings need your attendance and deserve your time.

- Make sure that meetings are properly chaired and that people have done the required homework.

- If the business is concluded or the meeting has filled its allocated time, end the meeting. The chairperson must ensure that essential business is covered in the time available.

- Question whether bringing large numbers of senior personnel together is necessary.

- Email minutes to people who were not present to keep them informed.

- When meeting clients away from the office, consider Smart Meetings technology.

# DRIVE THE CULTURE RIGHT THROUGH THE ORGANIZATION

ORGANIZATIONS CAN BE let down by the behavior of anyone within the organization at any level. We are all familiar with the bad impression created by poor service: an off-hand response to a complaint; an indifferent receptionist; an insensitive sales person; poor record-keeping. We do not conclude that is an unusual event and blame the individual concerned; we decide that the organization is not well managed. Leaders must drive a successful culture right through the organization.

## The idea

The cultural values of successful organizations tend to be established early on. Leaders are likely to find that they need to rediscover and re-emphasize the original values of an organization from time to time and to ensure that the values—the culture—are understood by everybody.

Sir Stuart Hampson, former chairman of the John Lewis Partnership, carried out extensive research across the organization. A set of very consistent values emerged: be honest; show respect; recognize others; work together; show enterprise; achieve more.

"They were not words that I had invented," said Hampson, "they were how everyone felt." Hampson makes the point that everyone within the company, at any level, should follow the spirit of the organization's culture. "Every one of us should operate those values at all levels; whether you are the chairman or whether you are working in one of the shops, it doesn't matter. Those principles apply every day to everything you do. The motivating and unifying effect of having said, those are the principles of the business and they characterize our behavior every day, has had a dramatic effect on the way we work together ... Creating a culture and distilling it into a form which everybody can understand, measure and talk about is a hugely unifying force."

## In practice

- Successful organizations have a culture that has helped to make them successful. The organization is damaged by anyone, at any level, who does not live up the organization's values and demonstrate them in their daily behavior.

- Leaders must distill the culture into a form that everyone can understand, and drive that culture through the whole organization—from the boardroom to the shop floor.

- A colleague who is unable or unwilling to operate within the values cannot stay with the organization, even if they are talented and apparently successful: their behavior will, at some point, clash with the organization's values.

# 45  ENCOURAGE DIVERSITY

DIVERSITY IN ANY ecosystem is essential to its survival: the different adaptations of various organisms within the system allow some to flourish when changing conditions condemn others to decline.

Organizations must encourage diversity, in terms of the people that they employ and the systems that they operate, to help them to adapt to increasingly rapid rates of change.

## The idea

When the intelligence centre at Bletchley Park was set up in the UK during World War II to decode enemy ciphers, it recruited people from a wide range of backgrounds, including mathematicians, chess champions, linguists and crossword puzzle solvers.

The different mental disciplines and abilities that each member of the team brought to the task enabled the dramatic breakthroughs that a team composed only of mathematicians, for example, might not have achieved.

As Gary Hamel, research fellow at Harvard Business School, highlights: "The diversity of any system determines its ability to adapt. Greater diversity—of thought, skills, attitudes and capabilities—equals a greater range of adaptive responses. The risk in a fast-changing world is that a company becomes over-adapted to a particular ecological niche ... As change accelerates, investing in diversity is not a luxury, it's a survival strategy."

Stuart Miller, former CEO and chairman of the energy exploration and marketing group, Royal Dutch Shell, talks of the benefits that come from working with a multi-national and multi-ethnic group of colleagues.

"You begin to find that you get some really neat ideas generated from creating a culture where people of different ethnicities, cultures, backgrounds [and] countries ... come together. Invariably, you find that the best ideas come from this mosaic of players working together in a team on a project. They will come up with an answer that is different from what any one of them would have come up with individually."

## In practice

- Organizations that are very homogeneous are badly equipped to deal with change: the skills and mental attitudes that have become entrenched in the organization are unlikely to deal well with changing situations and environments.

- There is an ingrained tendency to recruit people who will fit into the organization's existing culture: people who are "like us". Build teams of people with different attitudes, skills and experiences.

- Encourage the team to continue to broaden their experience whenever possible; create chances for them to learn about areas outside of their own specialization.

- Companies whose employees come from a wide variety of cultural and ethnic backgrounds provide the organization with a competitive advantage; a rich cultural mix tends to generate innovative approaches, and safeguards the organization against parochialism.

# ENCOURAGE INNOVATION

INNOVATION IS THE life-blood of all organizations. The right new idea could radically improve current processes or open up entirely new horizons.

## The idea

Whirlpool Corporation is currently the biggest home appliances manufacturer in the world.

In 1999, under the leadership of chairman and CEO David Whitwam, the company decided to make innovation central to its strategy. Whitwam decided that the company could no longer rely on big ideas requiring significant investment but with reasonably safe pay-offs as a source of successful new projects; he set out to encourage a large number of ideas, supported by relatively small initial funding.

Three Innovation Boards, whose job was to embed the idea of innovation into the organization, were created to allocate funding and to review processes. These were supported by a company-wide team of "I-Mentors" whose task was to make the knowledge and the tools needed for innovation available throughout the organization. The greatly increased number of ideas under discussion improved the likelihood of success; the cost of failure was acceptably low.

Whirlpool trained 22,000 employees to look for innovations in both products and internal systems. Senior executives were rewarded according to the number of ideas in the I-pipeline and its value. By

2006, the value of the ideas pipeline had grown from under $350 million to over $3 billion.

The executive charged with creating a new culture at Whirlpool with innovation at its core was Nancy Snyder, then director of strategy development.

Before the programme, says Snyder, "Innovation had been the responsibility of a couple of groups—engineering and marketing. Now, you have thousands of people involved. It's speeded things along. It's changed the focus of innovation to trying to deeply understand the customer and a belief that we could actually build customer loyalty in the appliance industry. That way we'll know if it's successful when it changes every job at Whirlpool."

Authors Mike Southon and Chris West write about the need to encourage an entrepreneurial mindset within large organizations. "Big companies fail to innovate well ... not because they are stupid, but because they are clever. So clever that they know their existing business superbly, and are caught on the hop by change." They recommend using the collective energies of the organization to address the challenge: "Look at every aspect of what you do, and ask, 'Can we let the imagination of our people loose on this?'"

## In practice

- Organizations have typically given a few people the task of testing and developing new ideas; encourage the whole organization to focus on innovation.

- Innovation needs support systems that will nurture a new idea and help its development. Make information and tools available.

- A truly effective innovation programme will affect everybody in the organization. Everybody will understand that innovation is key, and will know how to make a contribution.

- Don't allow the focus on essential core activities to blind you to other opportunities; let the imagination of your colleagues loose on possible opportunities.

# GET THE
# CULTURE RIGHT

THE CULTURE OF organizations is easy to recognize and hard to define. Positive cultures create an environment where success is encouraged, expected and celebrated.

Cultural defects can stifle optimism and ambition and undermine every new initiative.

Cultures tend to become established early on in an organization's history; to reflect the attitudes of the founders and the overall approach that made the organization successful in the first place. Changing an established culture is very difficult.

## The idea

Louis Gerstner achieved a remarkable turnaround of ailing computer giant IBM at a time when it seemed that the personal computer revolution would make IBM's core "mainframe" business outmoded and irrelevant.

Gerstner implemented wide-ranging programmes of management change, but also came to see that changing IBM's established culture was the most significant challenge.

"The hardest part of these decisions was neither the technological nor the economic transformations required. It was changing the culture—the mindset and instincts of hundreds of thousands of people who had grown up in an undeniably successful company, but one that had for decades been immune to normal, competitive and economic forces. The challenge was making that workforce live, compete, and win in the real world. It was like taking a lion raised for all of its life in captivity and suddenly teaching it to survive in the jungle."

Gerstner sets out his vision for the kind of high-performance culture that he wanted to achieve: "High-performance cultures are harder to define than to recognize. Once you enter a successful culture, you feel it immediately. The company executives are true leaders and self-starters. Employees are committed to the success of the organization. The products are first-rate. Everyone cares about quality. Losing to a competitor—whether it be a big fight or a small one—is a blow that makes people angry. Mediocrity is not tolerated. Excellence is praised, cherished, and rewarded."

"I came to see, in my time at IBM, that culture isn't just one aspect of the game—it is the game."

## In practice

- In any change programme, cultural issues will be more significant and more intractable than process issues. New systems and practices can be put in place, but the overall mindset of the organization will dictate the ultimate success or failure of these programmes.

- A good culture will be one in which the whole organization is deeply committed to the quality and excellence of products and services, to the performance of every member of the team and to the success of the organization.

- These values can be instilled and encouraged by the leadership, but must be reinforced by all of the organization's reward systems, in terms of both recognition and financial reward.

- A long and consistent leadership programme is needed to change a culture.

# HARNESS THE INTELLIGENCE OF THE ORGANIZATION

An organization's employees represent a pool of creativity that is at best only partially explored. People will bring their creative talents to their specified role but, as their private lives often demonstrate, they have a wide range of other talents and untapped creative energy to offer.

## The idea

Stephen Covey, management and leadership author, says that current research suggests that most people are far from fulfilled by their roles at work.

"The data is sobering. It matches my own experience with people in organizations of every kind all around the world ... Most people are not thriving in the organizations they work for. They are neither fulfilled nor excited ... Can you imagine the personal and organizational cost of failing to fully engage the passion, talent and intelligence of the workforce?"

Tony Fernandes, founder and CEO of low-cost Malaysian airline, AirAsia, says: "We're still a small operation, despite growing so fast, and that means everyone is valuable. At the end of the day, I would rather have 6,000 brains working for me instead of just 10. We are always innovating and we never stand still, and that has helped us. If there is a good idea, it can be implemented very fast as there is little bureaucracy. If there is a bad idea, we can kill it really fast too. That is how we do things that others may not try."

Computer giant IBM has demonstrated an interesting way forward with their "IBM Jams"—a series of web-based collaborative brainstorms designed to harness the ideas of as many of IBM employees and other stakeholders as possible.

In the 2006 Innovation Jam, more than 150,000 people from 104 countries and 67 companies gathered online. The ideas generated were freely available to anybody who chose to log on. IBM promised to invest $100 million in the most promising ideas and 10 new IBM businesses were launched as a result.

Google systematically encourages its employees to explore areas that are not in their official job description: things that they simply are interested in or feel passionate about.

As Google chairman and CEO Eric Schmidt says, "We're organized around something that's called 20 percent time, which means that engineers can spend roughly one day a week , which is a lot, to work on things that they find interesting. Most of our new ideas come from that 20 percent time."

## In practice

- People are ingenious and creative; much of this energy finds an outlet through their hobbies and other activities outside work. Find a way to harness some of this creative energy in your colleagues' working lives.

- The organization as a whole has more brains than the management team.

- Think about introducing set-piece events or ways of operating that systematically ask people to contribute their ideas. People will be energized by this process for its own sake—but be sure to reward successful contributions. Recognition may well be enough.

- Consider incorporating "thinking time" into people's job description.

# 49 HERDING CATS

ONE OF THE hardest leadership tasks is leading without the usual implied back-up of "command". People who are leading any kind of federation of equals do not have the same levers of power that are available to other leaders. It is more like "herding cats".

## The idea

Harvard Business School professor Allen Grossman spent six years as president and CEO of Outward Bound USA. His abiding interest is in the creation of high-performance non-profit organizations: "Someone described the task of running a federation as herding cats. The people in the organization were wonderful, but they had a deeply held cultural orientation for independence on the local level. I was the national CEO. I had to build consensus and convince local groups to agree that organizational change was not only in Outward Bound's best interest, but in their own self-interest as well. It was a really overwhelming and, at times, daunting challenge."

Narayana Murthy, co-founder and CEO of India's Infosys Technologies Ltd, helped to pioneer the Infosys concept of a Global Delivery System, optimizing costs and allowing around-the-clock project input from different time zones. Murthy describes a leader's role in bringing together many disparate elements of a loosely-bound organization as "telling a story" and "creating hope".

"The leader has to create hope. He has to create a plausible story about a better future for the organization: everyone should be able to see the rainbow and catch a part of it. This requires creating trust in people. And to create trust, the leader has to subscribe to a value system: a protocol for behavior that enhances the confidence, commitment and enthusiasm of the people. Compliance to a value system creates the environment for people to have high aspirations, self esteem, belief in fundamental values, confidence in the future and the enthusiasm necessary to take up apparently difficult tasks."

## In practice

- Some leadership tasks do not have the usual elements of direct management. Teams and individuals may not report directly to the leader, who therefore has no scope to influence behavior by means of the usual rewards and sanctions.

- In these circumstances, a leader relies on diplomacy and consensus-building and on agreement that success for the group as a whole results in success for the individual members of the group.

- This becomes challenging when the leader needs to instigate change at an organizational level in order to achieve greater success for the organization as a whole.

- Creating an overall value system, and a group "story" that people can engage with on a fundamental level, leads people to willingly take on tasks that move the organization towards its expressed goal.

# IMPLEMENTATION

YOUR COMPETITORS' STRATEGIES will be very much like your own. The organization that best executes its strategy will be successful.

## The idea

Frank Zhou, general manager of pharmaceutical company Abbott International China, argues that execution is especially important in markets such as China.

"My view is that in China, execution is a big issue. All the pharmaceutical multinationals have more or less similar strategies: They all know that China is a huge market, they all need to invest here and they all know we need to bring different product lines into China. However, what makes a company successful in the end is determined by whether or not it can be really good at doing what it wants to do ... In terms of accessing the market, retaining talent, establishing ethical standards and communicating with your head office, if you can do better than your competitors on these things, you will achieve better results ... We need to focus more on details, and to follow through and get things done."

As Jack Welch, previous CEO of General Electric, said, "I don't want to oversimplify strategy. But you just shouldn't agonize over it. Find the right aha and set the direction, put the right people in place, and work like crazy to execute better than anyone else, finding best practices and improving them every day."

## In practice

- You and your competitors are likely (for good reasons) to have similar strategies. The organization that executes its strategy best will succeed.

- The organization's strategy does not have to be radical or even original.

- How well the strategy is implemented is probably more significant than the originality or detail of the strategy itself.

# 51  MAKE SMALL IMPROVEMENTS

LEADERS WHO RELY on remarkable and spectacular successes as the route towards their goal are likely to be disappointed.

Steady, incremental improvements are more achievable and more reliable.

## The idea

Reuben Mark, former chairman and CEO of Colgate-Palmolive, led his company for a remarkably long period, serving 23 years as CEO and 22 years as chairman. He suggests that any company's progress should be targetted at small, incremental gains.

Using the analogy of the game of baseball, he argues that leaders should not rely on a spectacular but unlikely succession of dramatic successes—"home runs"; but on the steady accumulation of less spectacular results—"singles and doubles".

"The essence of leadership is the idea of continuous improvement. No matter what, you can always coach people to do a little better, and if everyone does that, the whole organization moves up ... It's not romantic and not revolutionary or headline-getting, but over time, that's what generates success."

Vikas Kedia is an India-born Internet entrepreneur who founded InterNext Technologies, based in Nevada, USA. After the unsuccessful launch of a software company to detect click fraud in online advertising, Kedia ran out of money. He found a job as a software designer, paid off his debts, and had the idea for developing an online community site that would allow people to share advice and information about their own financial problems online, in real time. Kedia highlights small improvements as one of the key means to achieving the successful new venture's monthly, tactical goals.

"We have strategic goals with us on what we are doing and why we are doing this. But we optimize our tactical goals on a monthly basis ... Within the organization, if we recognize that we can make small improvements we will do these. The idea is there is no one big thing that will get us where we want to get. There are actually a lot of small things that will help us to get where we want to get. So we keep on making the small improvements, keeping in mind the broader strategy."

## In practice

- Once the vision is established, it is more likely to be achieved by a series of small advancements than by dramatic leaps forward.

- Keep looking for any big breakthroughs that might be achievable, but look on a daily basis for small improvements that will move you towards your goals.

- Encourage an attitude and a spirit within the team that makes people feel that they have not had a successful day unless they have made some improvement to their part of the operation.

# MARCH TOWARDS THE SOUND OF THE GUNS

IN CORPORATE AFFAIRS it is essential to know where the main action is taking place, and to turn the organization in that direction. The organization must understand that this action is of vital importance to everybody and that jobs and the organization's entire future are potentially at risk; it needs to march towards the sound of the guns.

## The idea

In any battle, even with modern communications, events become confused. It may not be clear where the main action is or whether you are in the right position. A long-established piece of military advice has been to "march towards the sound of the guns". The gunfire clearly signals where an engagement is taking place; in the absence of any command to hold your position elsewhere, it is likely that you will be able to help by turning up at the scene of the fighting.

This advice holds true in business. Leaders often need to remind organizations that the action is not inside the comfortable corporate headquarters but outside somewhere, wherever customers are drifting away and competitors are stealing ground.

When Louis Gerstner was charged with turning around IBM in the 1990s, he felt that the company's long-established market dominance had taken the edge off its competitive spirit. He wanted his senior team to feel personally aggrieved about the damage that competitors in the burgeoning personal computer market were doing to IBM. He made a controversial speech to IBM's top management, pointing out that IBM's share of the market had halved at a time when the industry was rapidly expanding, and that customer satisfaction with IBM was dropping.

"I summarized those two snapshots of our collective performance by saying: 'We're getting our butts kicked in the marketplace. So I want us to start kicking some butts, namely, of our competitors ... We've got to create some collective anger here about what our competitors say about us, about what they're doing to us in the marketplace ... One hundred and twenty-five thousand IBM-ers are gone. They lost their jobs. Who did it to them? Was it an act of God? These guys came in and they beat us. They took that market share away and caused the pain in this company. It wasn't caused by anybody but the people plotting very carefully to rip away our business." Many IBM staffers were unhappy about the tone of this speech, but Gerstner was making a key point: organizations have to fight to survive.

## In practice

- Market changes are impersonal. The competition, on the other hand, actively wants to kill you. Both forces are equally deadly.

- This is not an academic exercise—jobs, livelihoods and even the future of the organization are at stake.

- Like armies, organizations must march towards the action: the battlefield is out there in the real world, not inside the organization.

# 53 MIX THINGS UP

ORGANIZATIONS NEED A constant flow of new ideas. Bringing together people from different cultures, experiences or fields of expertise creates an environment that is more likely to generate innovation.

## The idea

Frans Johansson, author of *The Medici Effect*, argues that innovation is encouraged when different cultures and ways of thinking come together to spark off new ideas. He recommends bringing together teams from diverse backgrounds and cultures and introducing new people to the team: many breakthrough discoveries are made by people who are either young, or who have recently moved into a new field of expertise; these people see things with fresh eyes.

Johansson cites a multi-disciplinary team of researchers at Brown University, Rhode Island, who pioneered research in using brain signals alone to control a cursor on a computer screen: the signals were interpreted using advanced statistical techniques, allowing the computer to turn the brain signals into workable instructions; the neuroscientists could not have done this without the statisticians or the other experts in the team.

In another example, a telecommunications engineer became intrigued by the way in which colonies of insects find the most efficient route to a source of food. His new understanding of biological mechanisms enabled him to find radical new solutions for the routing of electronic signals.

Jane Jacobs, a Canadian writer whose most influential book on urban planning, *The Death and Life of Great American Cities*, was published in 1961, was a passionate believer in the importance of diversity in urban areas. Jacobs argued that the existence of a variety of different kinds of buildings with different purposes within the same area—high- and low-rent residential properties, industrial and commercial premises, warehouses and artists' studios—creates a vibrant environment which brings many different kinds of people together and sets up the possibility of chance encounters and the exchange of ideas. Streets should be kept short; there should be many chances to turn corners, see new things and meet new people.

Jacobs used New York's Greenwich Village as a good example of a mixed urban community that has helped to create and support a successful and vibrant community.

## In practice

- Leaders need to create an environment in which the organization is constantly searching for better ways of doing things and new opportunities.

- Employing and bringing together people from different backgrounds, cultures and fields of expertise helps to create an atmosphere that encourages innovative ways of thinking.

- Move people around: find reasons to bring people together with new colleagues and different departments. Set up teams for special projects that come together and then disband, or teams that have a rapidly changing membership.

- Create spaces where colleagues can meet in unplanned ways.

- Broaden your own experience. Consider some apparently radical career options that would expose you to new ways of thinking. Take up new interests that take you away from your usual path.

# 54 NOT EVERYTHING IS MEASURABLE

Modern organizations may choose to operate in ways that would be condemned as inefficient by classic management theory. However, these chosen ways of doing business may give the company a competitive advantage.

## The idea

Gore Associates, the privately owned company that manufactures the waterproof and breathable fabric Gore-tex and many other polymer products, has always operated with an open and democratic system that asks colleagues to make a personal commitment to the projects they choose to work on.

The organization also chooses to base itself around clusters of individual plants that are near enough to allow easy communication, but which nevertheless operate as autonomous units. The company could make obvious savings by consolidating these plants into larger units.

Harvard Business School Research Fellow, Gary Hamel, has made a study of the operating systems of Gore Associates, and concludes that not all of the things that make the organization successful can be measured or quantified.

Although Gore's real estate arrangements could be rationalized to become more efficient, Gore themselves believe that "adjacency, autonomy and amity" are of vital importance: that having individual operating units, situated close to each other and in constant communication but still functioning as independent yet "friendly" units, is a very competitive way of running their business. This internal belief would be very hard to prove scientifically. It makes the associates at Gore happy and productive, but an external study would almost certainly conclude that this is an inefficient way to operate.

Hamel believes that there are "immeasurable" benefits that may allow a company to work in a uniquely competitive way.

"As we move towards a world in which economic value is increasingly the product of inspiration, mission and the joy that people find in their work, the sorts of management innovation that will be most essential are precisely those whose benefits will be most difficult to measure—an important fact for every management innovator, and every CEO, to keep in mind."

## In practice

- Management science has produced huge benefits for modern society by constantly improving the efficiency of modern manufacturing processes. No organization can survive in a competitive environment unless it operates in a fundamentally efficient way.

- Some organizations, nevertheless, may get a competitive advantage by encouraging human qualities that are difficult, or even impossible, to measure—such as a shared spirit of cooperation, endeavor and success.

- Encouraging these human qualities may demand operational conditions that are not as efficient as management science would require, but could still result in a competitive advantage.

- Modern organizations are unlikely to succeed merely by being more and more efficient; they will succeed by being more creative *and* more efficient. The conditions that encourage creativity may not appear to be the most efficient at first glance.

# 55 PLAN FOR EVERY CONTINGENCY

When making any important decision, it is a great advantage to have thought through, in detail, several possible options that best serve different likely contingencies.

## The idea

During his time at the Ford Motor Company, Lee Iacocca worked with Robert McNamara, who was to become Secretary of Defense under Presidents John F. Kennedy and Lyndon B. Johnson.

Iacocca describes McNamara as "one of the smartest men I've ever met, with a phenomenal IQ and a steel-trap mind. He was a mental giant. With his amazing capacity to absorb facts, he also retained everything he learned. But McNamara knew more than the actual facts—he also knew the hypothetical ones. When you talked with him, you realized that he had already played out in his head the relevant details for every conceivable option and scenario. He taught me never to make a decision without having a choice of at least vanilla or chocolate. And if more than a hundred million dollars were at stake, it was a good idea to have strawberry, too."

Richard Branson, chairman of Virgin Group, stresses the need to plan for the worst kind of contingency—a disaster: "You can take measures to mitigate and manage business risks. Then, if disaster strikes, at least your attention won't be split every which way by other worries. Always, always have a disaster protocol in place. Because if something truly horrific occurs, a lot of frightened people are going to come to you looking for answers."

Business author and Harvard Business School professor, John Kotter, warns against doing too much planning for the long-term, since something unforeseen will inevitably happen and the plans will have to be redone. Similarly, too much unguided short-term contingency planning can absorb a wasteful amount of management time.

"Short-term planning can become a management black hole, capable of absorbing an infinite amount of time and energy. With no vision and strategy to provide constraints around the planning process or to guide it, every eventuality deserves a plan. Under these circumstances, contingency planning can literally go on forever, draining time and attention from far more essential activities."

## In practice

- Plan for several contingencies. Hold as much information about these contingencies as you can in your head.

- Plan for disaster; even organizations that do not run the risk of a disaster that can affect its consumers still run the risk of a major incident, such as a fire. Have a business recovery plan in place.

- Don't waste much time on long-term contingency planning: something will change and the plans will be useless.

- Short-term contingency planning must be guided by the organization's overall direction: there is no point in planning for contingencies that are not relevant.

# 56 PRACTICE DEMOCRACY

---

FEW MODERN ORGANIZATIONS are run in a democratic way. Democratic process in organizations is not about the ballot box or making decisions by referendum, it is about harnessing the energies and creativity of the organization: creating an environment that favors change and adaptation, and that empowers and encourages colleagues to make a contribution.

---

## The idea

Gary Hamel, business author and research fellow at Harvard Business School, reminds us of a number of generally accepted truths about the modern world: the power of free markets and their ability to solve even the most complex allocation problems; the need for diversity within any ecosystem so that it can adapt to a changing environment; the need for individuals to work because they are motivated to improve their lives and not because they have been instructed to do so. These immensely powerful forces are still only imperfectly harnessed in modern organizations.

Hamel makes the point that there are very few perfect leaders, and that the great strength of democratic processes is that they compensate for this by leveraging the "everyday genius of ordinary citizens".

The real challenge for leaders is not so much to seek for perfection as leaders, but to set up structures that allow the organization to thrive with their less-than-perfect leadership. The key strength of democratic institutions is their capacity to adapt and evolve.

This, says Hamel, offers us some design rules for modern organizations: "Leaders must be truly accountable to the front lines;

employees must feel free to express the right of dissent; policy-making must be as decentralized as possible: activism must be encouraged and honored."

## In practice

- Democracy in organizations is not about deciding everything via the ballot box, it is about allowing the intelligence of the organization as a whole to influence the organization's future.

- Free markets and democratic institutions are infinitely adaptable. History demonstrates that attempts to run everything by central control fail disastrously.

- Leaders should not feel threatened by the process of democratization. The organization should be guided by the leader, not controlled.

- Colleagues must be invited to contribute and even to voice dissent, but nobody has the right to obstruct.

- Colleagues will feel empowered as their opinions are sought and incorporated into the organization's behavior.

- The organization, properly guided, will adapt to its environment in the most efficient way.

# 57 RESPECT THE CULTURE YOU INHERIT

EVERY ORGANIZATION HAS its own way of doing things; its own values and beliefs; its own culture. A new leader must respect this.

## The idea

Alan Mulally was appointed president and CEO of the Ford Motor Company after having spent all of his working life at The Boeing Company, where he was vice president of Boeing and CEO of Boeing Commercial Airplanes. He stresses the need to acquire a deep understanding of an organization before attempting to change it.

"I think any time you move into a new organization, it's just so important that you respect the history. You respect the people. You learn as much as you can about it. You seek to understand before you seek to be understood. And then you move very, very decisively but very sure-footedly into a new world. Because you know there is nothing worse than somebody coming in and acting like they know everything when you know they don't. They start handing out all of the assignments and it's just not the way I approach it. And the changes we've made: every one of them has been thoughtful, has been careful, and we've gotten a great response from the team."

Harvard Business School professor, Michael Beers, says that his research shows that effective leaders who move to a new organization should work with the materials that they are given; that they should adapt rather than destroy.

"Effective leaders build on what is already there. I know very few leaders who have succeeded in destroying the past. You have to honor the past ... That does not mean that [organizations] need to continue to do exactly what they did before. Yet leaders must recognize that the identity of people within the firm is critical to the recovery they are trying to fashion. Part of knowing who you are strategically, as well as from a values point of view, is finding a strategy to sustain. Always adapt, but don't destroy."

## In practice

- Leaders who move to new organizations should acquire a deep understanding of the organization before they try to change it.

- New colleagues will have spent their working lives immersed in that organization's history and culture; the new leader should learn as much as they can about this history and about their colleagues' perspectives before they embark on major change.

- Leaders should honor the past and adapt existing attitudes and processes to fit the new strategy.

- An organization can be led in a radically new direction and still retain its sense of identity. Some part of the organization's strategy and values should be carried forward in the new vision.

# 58 SERVANT LEADERSHIP

THE MODERN CONCEPT of servant-leadership was introduced by Robert K. Greenleaf in an essay written in 1970. Its central philosophy is that a leader's primary purpose is to serve the organization that they lead.

## The idea

Robert Greenleaf was inspired by *Journey to the East,* written by the mystical novelist Herman Hesse, author of *Steppenwolf, Siddartha* and *The Glass Bead Game.* Hesse himself was heavily influenced by Eastern philosophy; the concept of servant-leadership appears in early Indian Hindu texts, in Chinese Taoism and in Christianity.

As Greenleaf wrote: "The servant-leader is servant first ... It begins with the natural feeling that one wants to serve, to serve first. Then conscious choice brings one to aspire to lead. That person is sharply different from one who is leader first, perhaps because of the need to assuage an unusual power-drive or to acquire material possession ... The leader-first and the servant-first are two extreme types. Between them there are shadings and blends that are part of the infinite variety of human nature."

Colleen Barrett, former president of the USA's Southwest Airlines, has featured frequently in Forbe's list of the 100 Most Powerful Women. She has always described her leadership style as "servant-leadership". Customer service is her main priority, and she addresses this by ensuring that the organization delivers great service to its own workforce, on the assumption that a well-supported and highly motivated workforce will supply the best level of service to the company's customers. Barrett estimates that she spends 85% of her time working on staff and customer issues.

"When we have employees who have a problem—or have employees who see a passenger having a problem—we adopt them, and we really work hard to try to make something optimistic come out of whatever the situation is, to try to make people feel good whatever the dilemma is that they're dealing with."

## In practice

- The servant-leadership approach believes that a leader's primary concern should be to supply the organization with everything it needs in order to best carry out its purpose.

- Servant-leaders must ensure the organization understands that its primary purpose is to serve customers, and that every part of the team is focused on this.

- This is not an easy option for employees, despite the focus on staff support: the focus on the ultimate goal of excellent client service demands exceptional effort from every employee.

# 59 SET REASONABLE GOALS

It is one thing to have an inspiring vision—but can you achieve it? Leaders need to set challenging goals for the organization, but they have to be realistic. An unrealistic goal that the organization cannot achieve can lead to failure.

## The idea

John Chen, president and CEO of USA software services company Sybase Inc., says that it is essential to create a good match between an organization's ability and its vision.

"I think what I do best is to match reality with expectations—match the vision of what a company wants to achieve with its execution ability. It's not hard to have a vision, especially when you're in an industry long enough ... From talking to people and through experience, you inherently feel the pulse of the industry. That's why you're in the industry ... The question is, can you get from here to there? ... A lot of businesses fail for that reason. It's not because the individual CEO, president or management team isn't smart enough. It's because they aren't realistic enough."

Gregg Steinhafel is the chairman and CEO of Target Corporation, the USA's second largest discount retailer, behind Wal-Mart. Steinhafel says that the appropriate vision for Target is to be the best in other ways, not the biggest.

"We don't aspire to be as large as Wal-Mart; we know that's not going to happen. We want to be the best retail company we possibly can be. So we're focused on our demographics in servicing our guests the best way we possibly can. We know that if we can do that then we're going to be very successful as well. It's not a zero sum game. It's not as if Wal-Mart wins and everybody else loses. There's a lot of great retail companies and we believe that if we can effectively compete with Wal-Mart and stay true to our strategy, we will be highly successful over the next couple of decades."

## In practice

- Leaders should use their experience to set goals that challenge organizations to the limit of their ability, but not beyond.

- Having an ambitious and inspirational goal is not enough; leaders need to understand how the organization will achieve that goal. This involves a realistic assessment of the organization's capabilities.

- It is not essential to be the biggest or even the best. It is essential to deliver products or services extremely well, and to differentiate them sufficiently to command a place in the market.

- Leaders need to make a realistic assessment of what niche their organization can occupy and what it is capable of delivering.

# 60  ZERO TOLERANCE AND THE STAFF KITCHEN

IF THE TAP in the staff kitchen is broken and nobody mends it, colleagues begin to feel that the leadership does not care. Like fixing broken windows in a housing estate, mending small things that are broken helps to keep the sense of communal pride that people normally have in their environment.

## The idea

In a famous paper called "Broken Windows", the academics and political scientists, James Q. Wilson and George L. Kelling set out the idea that failure to mend small things in communal areas sends out a signal that nobody cares. Even normally well-behaved and law-abiding members of the community may join in destructive behavior as things begin to degenerate.

"Social psychologists and police officers tend to agree that if a window in a building is broken and is left unrepaired, all of the rest of the windows will soon be broken. This is as true in nice neighborhoods as in run-down ones. Window-breaking does not necessarily occur on a large scale because some areas are inhabited by determined window-breakers whereas others are populated by window-lovers; rather, one unrepaired broken window is a signal that no-one cares, and so breaking more windows costs nothing ... Untended property becomes fair game for people out for fun or plunder, and even for people who ordinarily would not dream of doing such things and who probably consider themselves law-abiding."

BBC Director General Greg Dyke put this kind of thinking into action when he decided to visit BBC offices outside London that were often overlooked by management.

"I went to BBC offices that no Director-General had visited in decades. I found that some of our staff were working in buildings that should have been condemned years earlier. I remember visiting our building in Leicester, the home of BBC Leicester and the Asian Network, and saying to people afterwards how awful it was. I was told that if I thought it was bad I should wait until I went to Stoke. When I finally visited Stoke I was pleasantly surprised; it wasn't that terrible. But over the next four years BBC Radio Stoke moved to a better building. We also moved to a new building in Sheffield and started work on replacement premises in Birmingham, Leeds, Hull, Liverpool, Glasgow, and finally Leicester. We also renovated buildings right across the country."

## In practice

- Small things matter. Colleagues will not be able to embrace new strategies or initiatives if some minor but significant aspect of their day-to-day working life convinces them that they are not valued.

- Letting small things go unfixed has surprising repercussions: previously well-behaved people begin to treat things with less respect, or even to indulge in minor acts of vandalism.

- Fixing the small things also has a disproportionate effect. A small amount of effort and expenditure convinces people that the leadership does, in fact, care.

# PART 5
# PERSONAL QUALITIES

# 61 BE AUTHENTIC

It is often believed that leaders need to control their emotions and to be able to present a "front" to their team which does not reflect their inner feelings. This has led to discussion about "the masks of leadership" and debate as to whether leaders can afford to be truly authentic.

## The idea

The concept of the "masks of leadership" belongs to a bygone age. Leaders must be authentic. People need to see the human process that has led a leader to their current position; only then can they genuinely believe in, and be inspired by, the leader's conviction.

Bill George, former chairman and CEO of Medtronics and co-author with Peter Sims of *True North: Discover your authentic leadership*, sets out five dimensions of authentic leadership.

1. Pursuing purpose with passion: a leader's passions demonstrate the true purpose of their leadership.

2. Practising solid values: integrity is required of every authentic leader.

3. Leading with the heart: authentic leaders lead with their hearts as well as their head.

4. Establishing enduring relationships: people demand a personal relationship with their leaders as a guarantee of trust and commitment.

5. Demonstrating self-discipline: authentic leaders set high standards for themselves and expect the same from others.

Dieter Zetsche, Chairman of Daimler AG and Head of Mercedes Benz Cars, puts the point succinctly: "You have to be the real deal. Don't pretend to be John Wayne if that description doesn't fit you. And if you are John Wayne, don't pretend to be Woody Allen."

## In practice

- Be guided by your passion: what you really care about is what you really want to do.

- Show integrity in all that you do; establish the organization's core values, promulgate them and live by them.

- Be prepared to share your human doubts, fears and uncertainties with your team; empathize with your colleagues; make decisions with your heart as well as your head.

- Allow colleagues to see you as a person and not only as a figurehead; leaders need to engage with people at an emotional level to be able to inspire trust and gain commitment.

- Be self-disciplined. Take responsibility and hold others accountable for their own decisions.

# 62 BE DECISIVE

THERE WILL NEVER be enough information to guarantee that you have made the right decision. At some point, leaders must trust their experience and their instinct and seize the moment.

## The idea

Making decisions is the defining aspect of leadership. There has never been a leader who made only right decisions. An effective decision made at the right moment is far better than no decision at all. A forceful exponent of this school of thinking was George S. Patton, the US Army General who led the armored dash across France towards Germany after Allied forces had established a beachhead in Normandy, in north-western France, in order to launch a land attack on Germany and bring an end to the Second World War.

His experiences in the First World War, during which he witnessed the futility of trench warfare, convinced him of the need to keep an attacking force constantly on the move. Patton was convinced that establishing a defensive line was what lost battles and got soldiers killed.

"Attack rapidly, ruthlessly, viciously, without rest—however tired and hungry you may be, the enemy will be more tired; more hungry." This aggressive, take-the-fight-to-the-enemy approach led to one of Patton's most famous quotations: "A good plan, violently executed now, is better than a perfect plan next week."

Lee Iacocca, president and CEO of the USA's Chrysler Corporation in the 1980s, offers a modern, corporate version of this philosophy:

"If I had to sum up in one word the qualities that make a good manager, I'd say that it all comes down to decisiveness. You can use the fanciest computer in the world and you can gather all the charts and numbers, but in the end you have to bring all your information together, set up a timetable, and act ... Too many managers let themselves get weighed down in their decision making ... at some point you've got to take that leap of faith. First, because even the right decision is wrong if it's made too late. Second, because in most cases there's no such thing as certainty."

## In practice

- Events move increasingly quickly; leaders do not have the luxury of waiting in order to make a better-informed decision.

- Delay can lead to the loss of a key opportunity or the establishment of a potentially overwhelming threat.

- With all of the information that is available to you at the time, with the advice of your peers and your organization, and based on your lifetime's experience, make a decision.

- Not to make a decision is a choice in itself. You are as accountable for non-decisions as you are for decisions.

- It is better to make a timely decision based on the best information available, and to repair any damage done later, if necessary, than not to make a decision and to be at the mercy of events.

# 63 BE FIRM

LEADERS NEED TO take firm action when standards have been allowed to slip, or when groups of colleagues attempt to get exceptional treatment by using their power or influence.

Leaders who are not firm will be perceived as being weak. People are resentful when a colleague's poor performance or exceptional treatment is overlooked. The organization begins to suffer.

## The idea

When Douglas Conant took over as president and chairman of Campbell Soups, the company was in trouble. Conant joined the company in 2001, after it had lost half its market value and been the worst-performing food company in the world for the previous four years.

"If you can imagine being in a troubled work environment for four years as an employee, seeing it go from bad to worse ... We had lost a lot of our best people and we needed to replace them." Conant took firm action. "I'm known around here as being very tough on standards but being tender with people. We had a level of activity and competence that was required to do the job, to dig ourselves out of the hole. People needed to get up to that—to that level of competence. If they couldn't, we'd help them find a role in the organization or outside the organization where they could succeed."

When television executive, Greg Dyke, became managing director of the British television franchise, LWT, he found that established union agreements were making it unaffordable to make programmes in-house. Greg told the team that unless the existing arrangements were changed, all future programmes would have to be made by independent producers. He reduced the standing workforce from 1,500 to 800, and embarked on a programme of discussions with groups of 20 colleagues at a time to explain why the changes were necessary for the company's survival. He offered generous redundancy terms to people who decided not to stay on under the new regime.

"One day I went to the leaving party of some videotape engineers who had earned fortunes in their time at LWT but who didn't want to stay on in the new world when their wages, and particularly their overtime, would be cut dramatically. They had decided to take redundancy instead. One of them summed up the past when he said quite openly to me, 'You can't blame us, governor. If the management were fools enough to give it, we were going to take it.' Who can disagree?"

## In practice

- No organization can be run without firm direction.

- Leaders should establish clear standards and benchmarks of behavior that must be seen to apply to every group and individual.

- If any group or individual is benefitting unfairly from a position of power or influence, every other member of the team feels disadvantaged.

- Practices that have become established may no longer be in the organization's best interests. People will want to continue as they have always done; it is a leader's job to be firm.

# 64   BE HONEST

HONESTY AND INTEGRITY are required of leaders in every situation and at all times. Two critical situations when honesty is especially needed are when colleagues must be told unwelcome news and when the organization must deal with presenting bad news to the outside world.

## The idea

Ram Charan, senior fellow at Wharton University of Pennsylvania and business author, stresses the need for realism and honesty in presenting difficult news to colleagues. This should be tempered with what he calls "grounded optimism"—a realistic appraisal of the facts, which encourages colleagues to rise to the occasion.

"You have tough and tenacious people working for you; engage them by putting the hard issues right in front of them. They will be motivated to overcome the challenges ... Leaders, wherever they sit in the organization, have to demonstrate rock-solid integrity, honesty, and the ability to confront reality. The way to inspire courage and optimism in your employees is by mapping a credible path forward. If you soft-pedal bad news, they won't trust you. Worse, they'll miss the urgency of the situation and won't follow you."

Narayana Murthy, chairman of India's Infosys Technologies, offers a clear message on how to present bad news to the outside world.

"Trust and confidence can only exist where there is a premium on transparency. The leader has to create an environment where each person feels secure enough to be able to disclose his or her mistakes, and resolves to improve. Investors respect such organizations.

Investors understand that the business will have good times and bad times. What they want you to do is to level with them at all times. They want you to disclose bad news on a proactive basis. At Infosys, our philosophy has always been, 'When in doubt, disclose'. ... Strong leadership in adverse times helps win the trust of the stakeholders, making it more likely that they will stand by you in your hour of need. As leaders who dream of growth and progress, integrity is your most wanted attribute. Lead your teams to fight for the truth and never compromise on your values."

## In practice

- Leaders must act with honesty and integrity at all times. When there is unwelcome news to disclose to colleagues, be honest and realistic.

- Give colleagues and stakeholders well-grounded reasons for optimism. Share with them your vision for how you will come through the current difficulties.

- If the company has news that will not be welcomed in the outside world, always disclose it. If you attempt to disguise or avoid releasing the news, it will eventually become public and you will be judged to have tried to cover it up.

- Investors and other stakeholders understand that mistakes happen and that companies go though good and bad times. The effect of any bad publicity will be temporary, provided that a plan for improvement can be seen to be in place.

## 65 BE HUMAN

WHILE THE ORGANIZATION does not want to see a leader's every passing humor, it does need to see his or her core, relevant emotions: passion, concern, dedication, hope, conviction.

At times the organization will want to see compassion and friendliness. Leaders also need to encourage the organization to explore its own humanity and to benefit from uniquely human talents such as creativity and ingenuity.

## The idea

Roger Ailes is a media advisor who worked on President George Bush's 1988 presidential campaign. He subsequently advised New York Mayor Rudolph Giuliani on his media presentation techniques and went on to become president of Fox News Channel and chairman of Fox Television Stations Group. Ailes advised Giuliani to stop reading his scripts to camera.

"Forget it. Just take your glasses off and start talking, and we'll get it right. If you feel angry, communicate it. Sad, communicate it. Mopey, communicate it. Let people know that you're a human being and the rest will take care of itself."

Jun Tang, Microsoft China President, reminds us that the workplace is not an emotionally neutral place where people assemble simply to make a living.

"In China, the company is as important as the family. When you have a problem, you can talk to your company management. If you are unhappy, you can discuss it with your colleagues."

Harvard Business School Research Fellow, Gary Hamel, makes a significant point: "There seems to be something in modern organizations that depletes the natural resilience and creativity of human beings, something that literally leaches these qualities out of employees during daylight hours. The culprit? Management principles and processes that foster discipline, punctuality, economy, rationality, and order, yet place little value on artistry, nonconformity, originality, audacity, and élan. To put it simply, most companies are only fractionally human because they make room for only a fraction of the qualities and capabilities that make us human. Billions of people turn up for work each day, but way too many of them are sleepwalking. The result: organizations that systematically under-perform their potential."

## In practice

- Do not try to turn yourself into a robot in the belief that your emotions are irrelevant or a distraction to your team. Let the team see your human qualities.

- The organization does not want to see your less noble emotions (spite, anger, frustration), but it welcomes the emotions that you bring to your role as leader: passion, hope, conviction, enthusiasm.

- Your team cannot be inspired by you if they cannot relate to you as a person. If you are undergoing an emotional experience—the birth of a child, pride in your family, a bereavement—share some of this with your colleagues.

- Emotions are not the only significant human qualities: try to harness the other human qualities of the organization: ingenuity, creativity, resilience.

# 66 BE PASSIONATE

PEOPLE ARE UNLIKELY to follow any leader who does not manage to convey the passion that they have for their cause. Leaders are also very unlikely to find the necessary energy and commitment needed to lead successfully unless they feel passionately about the field in which they work, and about the success of the organization that they lead.

## The idea

Richard Branson, chairman of Virgin Group, has always been driven in business by passion and excitement—by doing the things that interest him. This, in turn, is what makes him able to excite other people.

"At its heart, business is not about formality, or winning, or 'the bottom line', or profit, or commerce, or any of the things the business books tell you it's about. Business is what concerns us. If you care about something enough to do something about it, you're in business ... What really matters is what you create. Does it work or not? Does it make you proud?"

Harvard Business School professor, Allen Grossman, ex-CEO of Outward Bound, says that only genuine passion for what you do allows you to put in the hard work needed to ensure success.

"I haven't found a satisfactory substitute for just working your butt off. Virtually everyone I know, whether they be governor, president, the head of a public company, or whether they're at Harvard, Yale, or wherever, the common denominator is real commitment and focus. If you're not passionate, maybe self-discipline or whatever set of emotions you have, including guilt, might help you work hard. But most people who are really successful are also passionate. It is the wonderful ingredient that brings happiness with success."

Robert Mondavi, the California winemaker who helped to transform the reputation of North American wines, says that being passionate about what you do turns work into enjoyment.

"Interest is not enough. You must be passionate about what you do if your want to succeed and live a happy life. Find a job you love, and you will never have to work a day in your life."

## In practice

- If you are not passionate about what you do, you will not be able to bring other people with you; if your work does not fill you with excitement, you will not be able to find the energy for the hard work that your role as leader requires.

- Passion is not only about drive and ambition; it is about fun, excitement and self-fulfilment.

- Don't keep this passion to yourself: spread it around. Nothing is more infectious than a person's genuine passion for any subject.

# CONFIDENCE AND HUMILITY

LEADERS NEED TO tread a fine line between the need to have the necessary confidence that they are the person best suited to lead the organization, and the humility that will prevent them from imagining that they are in some fundamental way superior to the rest of the team.

## The idea

Rudolph Giuliani was mayor of New York City from 1994–2001. He makes the case for a leader's need for self-belief: "A leader has to have the confidence to think that his decisions will be proven correct. While trying to retain humility, you must accept that the reason you're making these decisions and other people are not is because, for now, you're in charge and they aren't. You do no one any good if, like Hamlet, you cannot carry the weight of your convictions. Yes, you must guard against arrogance; but if you're doing your job and putting your motive and conscience through their paces, accept that you really do know better and can see little further down the road than others."

John Chen, chairman, CEO and president of Sybase Inc., warns against arrogance.

"In the early days of my management career, I always thought everyone else was an idiot and I was so smart I just couldn't stand myself. I graduated from Caltech where we were brainwashed to think of ourselves as the top one per cent of the world. We were all very smart, but I have learned to be more humble. The more I achieve, the more I know the truth of the old Chinese maxim that says there are always higher mountains. It's absolutely true. There are always better people. There are always better minds. What you think you do best—and I think I do a lot of things well—there are always those who do it better. Nevertheless, I achieve a lot, and I am proud of my work for Sybase right now."

General Electric's Steve Schneider moved from the USA to Japan and then to China, where he was chairman and CEO of GE China. He confirms what was then a distinction between Western and Eastern management styles: "I grew up in the US system: things were black and white, arrogance was popular back then, 'take no prisoners' was popular back then. Everything was win-only, not win-win." Schneider says that he has now developed more humility and a more consultative leadership style. "It isn't a directive style; it's more of an influencing or coaching style. That's the way you get the best out of people."

## In practice

- Leaders cannot function without self-confidence. They have to believe, with justification, that they are the person best suited to make key decisions on behalf of the organization.

- This necessary self-confidence can easily flip into arrogance. An arrogant leader will fail to build a successful team.

- Successful leaders are confident in their abilities, but see themselves as team players and as enablers, influencers and facilitators rather than as commanders.

# 68 STAY ALERT

Leaders must stay alert to changes in the business environment; to the responses of customers and stakeholders; to the needs and reactions of colleagues.

Luckily, alertness is our natural response to fear, and leaders have plenty to be fearful about. Fear is a healthy response to new and challenging circumstances; it keeps us alert.

## The idea

John Sculley became CEO of Apple Computer in 1983, having previously been president of PepsiCo. Change and risk make us naturally fearful, says Sculley, but this is what keeps us alert.

"Anyone who is successful in business today must be able to deal in a risk environment, and I can't imagine they don't feel some fear in the process. Learning how to cope with your fear doesn't mean the fear goes away. It just means you learn how to succeed anyway, with it. That's probably positive in the sense that you remain alert, because in today's environment, things change so quickly—they can change day to day. What you thought were the ground rules for your industry one day can dramatically change the next because a competitor introduces a new product or the pricing structure shifts in the industry or scarce commodities suddenly become more scarce. These things happen instantaneously, so I think learning to live with fear and managing it is actually an important attribute to success. It's not something to be embarrassed about."

Jonathan Schwartz took over as CEO of Sun Microsystems when the company's co-founder, Scott McNealy, stepped down after 22 years at the helm, having helped to establish Sun in the 1980s as a major computing company and then successfully steered the company, as CEO, through the aftermath of the burst of the dot-com bubble in 2001. In an interview at the time, Schwarz acknowledged that taking over from McNealy—one of very few CEOs with a tenure of more than two decades—was difficult.

"It was terrifying. For me. Here is the guy who established a reputation and created the company that we are today, and [to] have him throw the keys to me and say, 'I'll talk to you in six months. Call me if you need me,' was pretty daunting. We have a perch in the industry, we have a presence and a reputation which I don't want to just uphold, I'd also like to amplify. Any new CEO who says he is not scared on the first day of his job is lying."

## In practice

- Leaders must cope with constantly changing circumstances and make decisions that involve risks. These things are frightening.

- Fear is a natural reaction. Successful leaders, like successful soldiers, acknowledge their fear and function with it.

- Any leader who is not experiencing some degree of fear is too complacent. There is always something to be scared of.

- Fear makes us alert, which is extremely useful. Alertness is a key leadership attribute.

# PART 6
# PERSONAL BEHAVIOR

# FOLLOW YOUR INSTINCTS

LEADERS ACQUIRE VERY good business instincts. These instincts represent the distillation of many years of experience, but they are often experienced as a kind of emotional reaction; a "gut feeling" that a decision is right.

Scientific evidence strongly suggests that we are right to trust these instincts: our emotional response system can be faster to make a "decision" than our conscious mind.

## The idea

Neuroscientists Antonio Damasio and Antoine Becher devised an ingenious experiment known as the Iowa Gambling Task. Volunteers were asked to pick cards from four separate piles; the cards awarded money prizes or exacted penalties but were rigged so that two of the stacks of cards offered relatively higher payouts but also occasional heavy fines. These piles of cards were the ones to avoid; playing the other stacks of cards produced a better overall result. The researchers wired up the volunteers to detect signs of stress and anxiety in the electrical conductance of their skin.

After only 10 cards had been drawn, volunteers showed signs of unconscious anxiety when they reached for cards from the "bad" packs. It took 50 cards before volunteers began consistently to draw cards only from the "good" packs; it took 80 cards before the average volunteer could explain why they were favoring the good packs. Our emotions can be faster to react than our conscious minds.

Richard Branson, chairman of Virgin Group, encourages leaders to engage their emotions at work: "Your instincts and emotions are there to help you. They are there to make things easier. For me, business is a 'gut feeling', and if it ever ceased to be so, I think I would give it up tomorrow. By 'gut feeling', I mean that I've developed a natural aptitude, tempered by huge amounts of experience, that tends to point me in the right direction rather than the wrong one. As a result, it gives me the confidence to make better decisions."

Anita Roddick, founder of the Body Shop, built the success of her cosmetics and body-care retail chain largely on her ground-breaking championship of social issues. The company struggled when it attempted to move into the USA market, and Roddick says that she failed to follow her gut instincts.

"Some people might say I interfere too much, but in America I felt I let myself be persuaded by others ... When sales began falling, we brought in a whole group of marketing people and product development people and they just looked around at what was going on in the marketplace and said we should do the same. I should have stepped in and told them that if that's the way the market is going, we should go in the opposite direction."

## In practice

- Our emotions, based on our experiences, are faster to react than our conscious minds; we feel scared or nervous before we can explain why, but for what turn out to be good reasons.

- Leaders should engage with their emotions at work: it is a mistake to believe that "cool, detached rationality" is the best way to approach every decision.

- You understand your organization better than nearly anyone else. Expert advice will be based on current realities, whereas your hunch about the future may very well be correct.

# LISTEN, LEARN AND ACT

LEADERS NEED TO listen to what colleagues, customers and any other interested party is saying, and to learn from what they hear. It is essential to understand the other person's point of view. Showing team members that you have listened, understood and acted is very motivating.

## The idea

Wu Xiaobing, president and MD of pharmaceutical company Wyeth China, has worked in different countries and different cultures. He believes in the need to "listen, adapt, understand and learn".

"Everyone has challenges. I had a lot of challenges and they are still coming continuously. If you look at my experience ... I have worked in various countries and grown up in a different cultural background ... The biggest thing is that you have to listen, adapt, understand and learn constantly; don't take it for granted that you are necessarily right. You need to listen to others sincerely, to understand why he says things differently. When someone challenges your argument, he has his own reasoning. You have to understand his reasons."

Alan Mulally, president and CEO of Ford Motor Company, talks about how listening and taking action as a result is immensely energizing for the team. Ford's senior management hold weekly business-plan review meetings that cover the company's global operations.

"And it's very interesting because we invite guests every week to the business-plan review ... They could be in assembly. They could be in finance. They're from all across Ford worldwide. Then we invite them in as guests. We introduce them as guests of the leadership team ... And then at the end of the meeting we go back around through the guests and we ask the guests for their feedback for what they thought. I know it is the most incredible experience, it makes your eyes water ... We had, I think, on one of those meetings about the launch of that vehicle, we had one of the assembly workers that was going through that process and she said, 'You know, this is so exciting because what you are looking at here with that red is exactly where I am and it is red [Mulally had introduced a "traffic light" system for the review meetings that would flag up progress on any project as red, amber or green], but I know that we are getting help now because you know it, we know it; you listened to us.'

## In practice

- Listen to what anyone has to say; understand his or her point of view; learn and adapt.

- Create situations that prove you are listening: set up systems that flag up potential problems; invite colleagues to senior meetings; show that you are aware of the issues; make help available.

- Show the team that they are allowed to have problems and that the organization will supply them with the necessary help and support.

- This open attitude will create a "can-do" problem-solving atmosphere.

# SAY SORRY SOMETIMES

WE WORK INTENSIVELY with our colleagues. Very few leaders will be able to search their hearts and feel that there are not some colleagues to whom they should have said "sorry" on occasions. An apology is a powerful thing that can only improve your relations with your colleagues. Saying "thank you" is pretty good too.

## The idea

Marshall Goldsmith is a successful executive coach and business author. He argues compellingly that it is behavioral issues that prevent people from reaching their full potential: anyone who is near the top of their profession has already proven their skills and abilities; it is the way in which they relate to their colleagues that may limit the level of leadership to which they can aspire. His typical coaching technique is to use in-depth 360 degree feedback from executives' colleagues to identify problem areas. Once an executive had acknowledged the need for change (and the great advantages that change will offer), then saying "sorry", says Goldsmith, is the most important next step.

"I regard apologizing as the most magical, healing, restorative gesture human beings can make. It is the centrepiece of my work with executives who want to get better—because without the apology there is no recognition that mistakes have been made, there is no announcement to the world of the intention to change and most importantly there is no emotional contract between you and the people you care about. Saying you're sorry to someone writes that contract in blood."

Goldsmith is talking here about a formal process of behavioral change, which few of us undergo. But it is unlikely that there is not some working relationship you have with a colleague that would not be improved by saying "sorry" for an act or omission of yours.

## In practice

- We work closely with our colleagues and have a personal relationship with them.

- We are reluctant to say sorry, but we should not be. Apologizing makes our working relationships better; it acknowledges that leaders are not infallible and creates an emotional bond.

- Because we are all human, it is highly likely that something that a leader has done will have caused unnecessary upset to a colleague.

- Saying thank you is also easy and equally important. A small gesture of thanks can have a disproportionate effect.

# 72  SET A GOOD EXAMPLE

ONE OF THE most difficult aspects of being a leader is that you are constantly on show. Everything that you do is seen by the organization and by a wider public. Leaders have no option but to set a good example in everything that they do.

## The idea

Sir John Harvey-Jones, previous chairman of UK chemical giant ICI, points out that the organization may read significance into what is, in fact, a moment of irritation or a bad mood, and that it is dangerous to appear in public when one is not at one's mental and physical best.

"One of the penalties of leadership is indeed that people watch your mood in a way which you do not allow for ... I remember another occasion on which, in my anxiety to ensure that I spoke to a management course, I came straight off the overnight plane from America to address them. I barely had time for a shave before I appeared ... I felt very virtuous and proud until I got the feedback, which was that they were concerned that perhaps I was losing my grip! Entirely my own fault, but it certainly taught me not to assume that one can perform tasks beyond one's physical capability."

Reuben Mark, previous chairman and CEO of Colgate-Palmolive reminds us that a corporate leader's integrity must be unquestionable and that leaders must demonstrate integrity in all things, not just in major issues of corporate governance. Leaders cannot be seen to be "bending the rules".

He highlights the case of Tyco chief executive Dennis Kozlowski, who paid restitution for tax evasion after admitting that works of art that he had declared to be for the company's use were in fact on display in his New York apartment. Empty cartons supposedly containing the artworks were sent to a warehouse. Mark talks about the impact on a worker handling those empty cartons: "He knows that the boss is cheating on taxes. How can you really expect that warehouseman to be honest in his job when the example he's getting is just the opposite? With everything you do as a leader, you've got to think not only, 'Is it the right thing for me to do?' but, 'Is it right for the organization?'"

## In practice

- Setting a good example applies as much to relatively unimportant issues, such as the impression that you gave at the last presentation, as it does to serious issues about your personal behaviour.

- Leaders must try to avoid seeming bad-tempered, irritable or moody since people are likely to interpret this as being significant.

- Avoid taking on more than you are physically capable of.

- Integrity on major issues of governance is taken for granted. Integrity on lesser issues is just as important. If a leader bends the rules, the team will assume that they can do the same.

# 73  STICK TO THE STRATEGY

STICKING TO THE strategy gets difficult when it involves, for example, not retaining a major contract or not taking up an attractive opportunity outside the organization's agreed area of activity.

## The idea

Narayana Murthy is the founder of Infosys Technologies, the global IT services company based in India.

Early in the company's history, Murthy decided not to accept the tough terms sought by a client which accounted for one quarter of all of his company's current revenue.

"Our various arguments why a fair price—one that allowed us to invest in good people, R&D, infrastructure, technology and training—was actually in their interest, failed to cut any ice with the customer ... Through many a tough call, we had always thought about the long-term interests of Infosys. I communicated clearly to the customer team that we could not accept their terms, since it could well lead us to letting them down later. But I promised a smooth, professional transition to a vendor of the customer's choice. This was a turning point for Infosys."

Lui Chuanzhi is co-founder of Lenovo Group, a China-based computer manufacturer. During the company's period of dramatic growth in the mid-1990s, Chuanzhi faced many core-strategy decisions.

"When Lenovo gained recognition in the market and from society, many people asked us to do more core technology, which was the most profitable item in the value chain and was controlled by companies [such as Intel] in developed countries. After thorough research, we determined not to do that."

With real estate values in China booming, many companies also diversified into land and property. "We began to discuss internally whether should we buy land here and there. But we didn't feel good about that strategy ... The conclusion was that we should focus on computers. There were always too many temptations ... We are happy that although we haven't done everything, we have accomplished some things that we wanted to do. [Having] clear strategies made us focused."

## In practice

- There will always be temptations to deviate from the agreed strategy, either to keep current revenue or to make significant new revenue in a different business area.

- The decision to keep existing business at any cost represents a change of strategy: reducing prices may lead to reduced levels of investment and service.

- There are always new money-making opportunities. The apparent gains have a cost in distracting the organization from its agreed purpose.

- Strategies that have been carefully considered and debated in depth with colleagues should not be changed for short-term gain.

# 74 STICK TO THE VALUES

An organization's values dictate how the organization deals with its members and customers and with the outside world in general. Ensuring that everyone in the organization adheres to those values guarantees that colleagues behave appropriately towards each other and towards customers, and that business is conducted in an ethical and honest manner wherever it operates.

## The idea

Gerard Kleisterlee, president and CEO of Philips, the multinational Dutch electronics company, talks about how the company's values transcend national borders: that they must apply to any market in which the company does business.

"In 2001/2002, we updated our values. We describe them today as the four Ds—we delight our customers, deliver great results, develop our people, and depend on each other. Although we have not formulated any typical values, things like business ethics, integrity, honesty, and so on are all part of our business principles. We believe that they are self-evident. But the four 'Ds' are our transcendent culture, be it in Asia, the United States or Europe."

Kenneth Yu, Managing Director of 3M China, points out that in the early days of the company's operations in China, the country's environmental laws were less strict than they were in the United States, so that it would have been quite legal for the company to relax its usual environmental policies. The company decided to stick to its values and its standard procedures, even though this cost them business at first.

"In the early days, people said when you do business in a developing economy, you do it differently ... but when it comes to business ethics, there is no compromise ... We did lose business in the early days. We'd rather lose a customer than taint our squeaky-clean image ... Environmental law here, although it is getting tougher, isn't like in the US. At the beginning, we raised eyebrows. Over time it has given 3M a lot of good publicity, and we eventually got benefits from the host government in the area."

## In practice

- An organization's values dictate how it deals with its own members, with customers and with the outside world. It is the leader's job to make sure that those values are clearly understood throughout the organization and that they are not forgotten.

- It should not be necessary to remind colleagues to do business in an ethical way, but leaders must ensure that basic standards of honesty and integrity never slip.

- International organizations will do business in places with different cultures and legislation. The company's values should not change in different contexts.

# 75 STICK TO THE VISION

THE VISION OF an organization can be quite simple, but the right vision has a profound effect on the organization's behavior, and can guide it through periods of great change and difficulty.

## The idea

Ruben Vardanian is chairman and CEO of Troika Dialog, Russia's leading private investment bank. When the company was founded in 1991, its guiding vision included principles that would guide the company through the turbulent times following the dissolution of the Soviet Union and the founding of the Russian Federation, as the old government planning system was replaced by free financial markets.

The company established core principles from the outset: to position itself for the long-term and as a client service organization and to benchmark the company against international standards. It was the only investment bank in Russia to employ external auditors to report on their first year's losses. The company turned down business from clients who were being offered very high guaranteed rates of return by other investment companies.

"Looking back today, that seems easy to say, but at the time it was quite tough. We didn't know if we would have money to pay salaries at that time. But I knew it would be wrong, and I knew sooner or later we would be paid back for it. This is why you need to have a dream. You need to have a vision ... You need to understand what kind of things you will do and what kind of things you will not do."

Andrea Jung, chairman and CEO of Avon Products Inc, talks of the company's vision, dating back to its founding in 1886, which was to empower women to run their own independent businesses under the Avon banner.

"The whole legacy that comes with being 122 years old has good and bad aspects. Now that we're a $10-billion-plus company there is a completely different set of requirements. Running the company today is completely different; the global marketplace is different; the competition is different; the consumer is different; the selling requirements for our Representatives are different. Everything has changed around the company—except, luckily, the original mission. So I as the CEO have always to ask myself how I can make sure the company stays fit for the future without neglecting its heritage and its history. ... It is a unique thing to have a founder who believed in 1886 that women, who could not even vote at that time, should be empowered to run their own independent businesses ... luckily through all the decades of the company and all the transitions, that has remained the constant vision."

## In practice

- The right vision will help to guide an organization through difficult times and help it to make the right decision.

- Part of a leader's role is to interpret the vision for current conditions and to present it to colleagues in contemporary terms.

- The vision will guide leaders and the organization though periods of great change; everything else may be altered and developed, but the vision remains the same.

# 76 STOP BEING JUDGEMENTAL

It is very easy for leaders to pass judgement on colleagues. To some extent this might be seen to be part of a leader's brief. In fact, being judgemental switches colleagues off more effectively than any other leadership error, and achieves almost nothing positive by way of compensation.

## The idea

Leadership development consultant and author, Marshall Goldsmith, lists "passing judgement" as one of the unconscious bad habits that prevent us from being better leaders.

He recommends a test: "For one week, treat every idea that comes your way from another person with complete neutrality ... Don't take sides. Don't express an opinion. Don't judge the comment." Goldsmith recommends that we simply say "Thank you". This will greatly reduce the amount of time spent having pointless arguments with colleagues, he says. More importantly, "people will begin to see you as a much more agreeable person, even when you are not in fact agreeing with them. Do this consistently and people will eventually brand you as someone whose door they can knock on when they have an idea." Similar "judgemental" bad habits listed by Goldsmith include routinely starting our sentences with "no", "but", or "however" or, in effect, "let me explain why that won't work".

Morgan McCall, business author and professor at the Marshall School of Business has written about "why leaders derail". He interviewed the peers and colleagues of apparently successful leaders whose careers had come to a sudden end.

"Insensitivity was the most commonly reported flaw among derailed executives in our research and one of the sharpest differentiators between derailed and successful executives. Humiliating managers in front of peers or subordinates, cutting people off, demeaning others' ideas—everyone who has ever worked for an insensitive boss ... knows the story and the incredible visceral response such treatment generates. Power and intimidation can produce compliance, but insensitivity can lead to lack of support at crucial junctures, failures of subordinates to pass on important information, active sabotage, loss of ideas from below, and a host of counterproductive activities. Organizations seem quite willing to overlook the flaw of insensitivity as long as someone gets results, but at the higher levels of management, alienating people in most cases assures that good results will not be sustained over time. It can't be very useful to have large numbers of people eager to see one fail."

## In practice

- Passing judgement is something we all do without thinking; we feel obliged to make our views known. This is not helpful and can have negative effects.

- Practice being neutral. When people bring ideas and comments to you, just say "Thank you".

- Look out for other habitual negative responses that are, in effect, judgemental.

- Leaders who are judgmental to the point of being insensitive, and even abusive, lose all support. This limits their effectiveness.

- Insensitive and judgemental behavior can reach a critical point, at which leaders can suddenly be asked to step down.

# 77 USE SYMBOLS

An organization's vision should be clear, simple and easy to explain. The various strategies that it uses in order to achieve the vision may be more complex, but they must still be understood by everybody. A symbol, image or metaphor is always easier to understand and remember than a detailed argument.

## The idea

Franklin Delano Roosevelt served four terms in office as President of the United States of America, from 1933 to 1945; the only American president to serve more than two terms. Roosevelt's long presidency began in the Great Depression and continued throughout World War II.

In these turbulent times, Roosevelt made great use of the media, and in particular of the relatively new medium of radio, to address the American public. He made very effective use of metaphors to get his point across, comparing significant national issues to relatively minor domestic crises in a way that was easy to understand and remember.

In 1941, Britain could no longer afford to pay for the arms and munitions that America had been supplying to support Britain's war with Nazi Germany, but a 1934 Act of Congress prevented America from trading with any other warring nation other than on cash terms. Johnson invented the notion of "Lend-Lease" and sold this to the American public in a disarming way: "Suppose my neighbor's home catches fire, and I have a length of garden hose four or five hundred feet away. If he can take my garden hose and connect it up with his hydrant, I may help him to put out his fire ... I don't say to him before that operation, 'Neighbor, my garden hose cost me $15; you have to pay me $15 for it.' I don't want $15—I want my garden hose back after the fire is over."

Similarly, when the American government needed to sell a record number of War Bonds to finance the continuing war, Roosevelt drew on the image of a community piling sandbags onto the levees of a swollen river to save the town from flooding.

"Today, in the same kind of community effort, only very much larger, the United Nations and their peoples have kept the levees of civilization high enough to prevent the floods of aggression and barbarism and wholesale murder from engulfing us all. The flood has been raging for four years. At last we are beginning to gain on it; but the waters have not yet receded enough for us to relax our sweating work with the sand bags. In this War Bond campaign we are filling bags and placing them against the flood."

## In practice

- When addressing large groups of people, keep the message simple.

- Make use of metaphors, symbols and images to get the message across. These are more easily grasped and remembered.

- The central image or metaphor is what will be remembered. The team should have some record of the detail that they can refer to when necessary.

# PART 7

# PERSONAL DEVELOPMENT

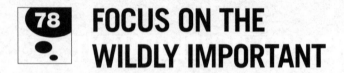

# FOCUS ON THE WILDLY IMPORTANT

It is easy to become distracted and even overwhelmed by the sheer number of things that apparently have to be done. Highly effective leaders focus on a small number of core goals that will have a significant effect on a wide range of other targets.

Concentrating on these "wildly important" issues clears the mind and is a key factor in achieving improved productivity and a better work-life balance.

## The idea

Stephen Covey, management and leadership author and co-founder of the FranklinCovey Company, says, "You need to narrow your focus down to the one, two or three most important goals you must achieve. These goals are so important that if you don't achieve them, nothing else you achieve really matters much."

This kind of prioritization, says Covey, is essential for effective leadership, and should also cascade through the whole organization.

"The bottom line is, when people are crystal clear about the most important priorities of the organization and team they work with and [have] prioritized their work around those top priorities, not only are they many times more productive, they discover they have the time they need to have a whole life."

Progress towards achieving the key goals must be measurable; key activities that demonstrate progress towards achieving the core goals should be selected and monitored weekly.

Martha Lane Fox, co-founder of lastminute.com, talks about the need for leaders to "get out of the detail" to focus on the really important issues.

"Good leaders know when to get into the detail and know when to get out of it again. I often see people who immerse themselves in detail for comfort. They busy themselves with meetings and all the things you need to do daily in a business while being too scared to think, 'What could really transform this business?' or, 'What direction is this business going in five, 10 or 15 years time?' Mind you, in lastminute.com's time frame, it was five, 10 or 15 months' time."

## In practice

- Focus on the core achievements that are most essential to achieving your overall goals. Choose not more than three "wildly important" goals.

- Ensure that the team understands these goals and prioritize their own activities to focus on achieving the core overriding goals.

- Choose key measures that will indicate progress towards achieving these goals; monitor progress and make the results visible to everyone as frequently as possible—ideally weekly.

- Step back from the detail of the job whenever possible; changing circumstances will affect what needs to be done to achieve the goals.

- Successful prioritization will improve the efficiency of the organization as a whole and free up everyone's time, improving productivity and work-life balance.

# GET A GOOD PA

LEADERS MUST KEEP their desk and their minds as free from routine issues as possible. A really good personal assistant is essential.

## The idea

Ken Davenport is a Broadway producer. When he first started his own production company he worked out of his apartment, but soon found himself running a growing organization. This began to stop him from doing what he was best at: dreaming up new projects and driving the organization forward.

"One of the greatest challenges entrepreneurs and business founders face is finding a way to keep up the creativity that started their company as the day-to-day grind of running it gets more and more cumbersome ... The right assistant can save you hours every day. Every minute saved can be put into new projects and, maybe, just maybe, a moment to relax. Conversely, the wrong assistant can cost you hours a day. Don't skimp. Get someone with experience."

Vanessa Cameron is the chief executive of the Royal College of Psychiatrists in London. Her role involves a great deal of national and international travel, and she relies on her assistant to coordinate both her diary and her itinerary. Far more than this, she relies on her PA as her confidante—perhaps the only person in the organization who will give her a genuinely frank opinion and who knows her well enough to notice, for example, that she is under stress, or that she has taken the wrong tone in a particular communication.

"My PA is my right hand. She is someone in whom I have absolute trust. I can rely utterly on her loyalty but, more importantly, I know that she will always tell me the truth—rather than telling me what she thinks I want to hear. She will also tell me when she thinks I am doing something wrong. She will change my letters if I have got the wrong tone—too aggressive, or too apologetic, or if the facts are wrong ... She knows when I am under stress and reacts accordingly."

## In practice

- A leader's role is to direct and guide the organization, not to administer it.

- One of the key skills of successful leaders is the ability to choose where to focus their time, rather than being at the mercy of their diary.

- A good personal assistant can be charged with significant decisions about what is and is not essential for the leader's attention and time. They can also take care of a great deal of time-consuming detail and can help the leader in the delegation of tasks to other team members.

- A top-flight assistant can provide leaders with an objective commentary on their behavior; it is not possible to have this kind of relationship with any other member of the team.

# 80 GET A LIFE

LEADERS NEED A life outside work. Working too many hours is counter-productive; quality of work and one's perspective on life both suffer.

Lack of healthy social and family relationships can cause leaders to behave badly and to make poor ethical decisions.

## The idea

Tom Stern used to be a stand-up comic; he then launched a highly successful executive search company and found himself so driven by his urge to succeed that his family life suffered. He now considers himself to be "a recovering success addict".

"People who work too much tend to have really bad personal lives. Their families become unhappy, their children have problems that are distracting and emotionally draining, their wives are angry all the time. Obviously, job performance suffers. It's not just how many hours you're putting in or how much you're churning out. There's the quality of your work. And studies show that compulsive workaholism does not produce a better product ... I believe the family is a grounding mechanism. Your family will talk to you in a way people never would in business, especially if you're a high-level executive ... If you're not connecting with your family, you don't have that critical grounding mechanism. And for certain personalities, that can lead to immense arrogance and ethical management issues."

Sharon McDowell-Larsen of the Center for Creative Leadership is a former US Olympic Committee researcher. She reminds us that, in business as in sport, "recovery time" is essential: "Learn from professional athletes. You can actually do more in less time by practicing the art of recovery. Professional athletes understand that pushing themselves at 100% of their capacity 100% of the time results in little or no long-term performance gain. They build time to recharge into their training routines. You can do the same. Do it by finding effective ways to set boundaries. Listen to music on your commute home. Turn off your cellphone and your e-mail during personal or family time. Take up a social activity or a hobby. Relaxing is critical for clear and creative thinking, strong relationships and good health. Know that the time and energy you spend away from work can enhance your productivity and your capacity to deal with things at work."

## In practice

- Keep an eye on the hours that you are working—at home as well as in the office.

- Lack of good social relationships is not some kind of unavoidable collateral damage that goes with being successful. Apart from the damage that you are doing to other people, you are damaging your own mental health and your effectiveness as a leader.

- The lack of any balancing input from healthy social relationships can lead to insensitivity and arrogance, which leads to bad decision making and even ethical lapses.

- Leaders need time to relax and reflect. Minor changes in routine can be very effective: use travelling time to "switch off"; make sure that you are not distracted when you are with your family or friends; take up a hobby.

# GET OUT OF
# THE LIMELIGHT

Leaders can find it difficult to stop themselves from making a contribution to colleagues' ideas because they feel the need to offer the benefit of their own knowledge and expertise.

The benefit of giving this advice may be outweighed by colleagues' perception that they have lost ownership of the idea.

Some leaders also feel the need to demonstrate why they are the leader and to indulge in competitive behavior.

## The idea

Executive coach and business author, Marshall Goldsmith, says that leaders, understandably, feel the need to demonstrate why they are the leader, and to offer the benefit of their knowledge and experience on every occasion. Goldsmith calls this "adding too much value":

"Imagine you're the CEO. I come to you with an idea that you think is very good. Rather than just pat me on the back and say, 'Great idea!' your inclination (because you have to add value) is to say, 'Good idea, but it'd be better if you tried it this way.' The problem is, you may have improved the content of my idea by five percent, but you've reduced my commitment to executing it by 50 percent, because you've taken away my ownership of the idea."

Goldsmith also identifies "winning too much" and "telling the world how smart we are" as unconscious habits that hinder a leader's relationship with the team. Leaders are competitive by nature, but they don't need to win at their colleagues' expense or to blow their own trumpets. Leaders often fail to address behavior of this kind because they see it as being part of what makes them successful: "it's just the way I am". Goldsmith identifies this as a problem in itself: "the excessive need to be me".

## In practice

- We all have minor behavioral defects. In a leader, these can greatly reduce their effectiveness and the ability to inspire others.

- A lot of these behavioral patterns stem from an instinctive need to "steal the limelight"; to be seen to be the leader.

- This ineffective behavior is often seen as "just the way we are" but it reduces colleagues' levels of motivation.

- Leaders should not prove themselves by indulging in competitive behavior at colleagues' expense. Allowing colleagues to have self-confidence and to get their own share of the limelight is a key part of successful leadership.

# GOOD ENOUGH

LEADERS SHOULD PURSUE excellence but be wary of perfectionism. It is more important to get a product out into the market in a timely way than it is to wait until that product or service is "perfected".

The benefits of the last refinements are likely to be greatly outweighed by failing to release something when the market is ready and before the competition can move in.

## The idea

Sir John Harvey-Jones, ex-chairman of ICI, makes the point very well: "Remember that the best is a relative not an absolute measure. The standards of the best are set by the competition and one's aim is always to exceed them. However, as in many other aspects of business management the best, if sought in absolute terms, is the enemy of the good."

Business authors Mike Southon and Chris West have written about the need for companies to adopt more of the attitudes and techniques of entrepreneurs. They warn of the tendency (amongst entrepreneurs, as well as others) towards perfectionism: "Many entrepreneurs are passionate custodians of 'brand value'. While they are right up to a point to be so, beyond this point they are wrong: waiting for perfection can cause fatal delay ... A mentality develops—'Just wait until we've fixed the X problem'—which puts the rest of the business into paralysis."

In the 1990s, the giant mainframe computer manufacturer IBM, was in trouble. The new personal computer was revolutionizing the market, and IBM was seen as being large, bureaucratic and slow to react. The company was obsessed with perfecting its products before release, to the detriment of successful marketing. An insider joke at the time was: "Products aren't launched at IBM. They escape."

IBM staffers John Patrick and David Grossman played a fundamental role in introducing IBM to the potential benefits of the emerging world wide web. They built what was then the world's biggest website for the 1996 Summer Olympics, in the face of considerable resistance from some of their senior colleagues, who were institutionally resistant to "trying something out" in public. But with the Internet, problems could be fixed in real time on the server. Patrick and Grossman introduced a set of new principles for the growing community of IBM web developers, which included: Start simple, grow fast; Just don't inhale (the stale air of orthodoxy); Take risks, make mistakes quickly, fix them fast; Just enough is good enough; Don't get pinned down (to any one way of thinking).

## In practice

- Organizations must release products and services at the right moment that are good enough to attract customers.

- Leaders should encourage a culture that embraces change and experiment: "perfectionist" cultures see change and experiment as risks to an idealized brand.

- Products can be developed and improved over time; the search for perfection before launch can be at the expense of the ideal window of opportunity.

- The pursuit of excellence must not be allowed to prevent experimentation or to slow the organization down.

# KEEP A SENSE OF BURNING URGENCY

LEADERS NEED TO transmit their own sense of urgency to their colleagues. There is a great deal to achieve and a limited amount of time; it is essential that leaders impress their sense of urgency on the team from day one.

## The idea

Ex-chairman and CEO of Schering-Plough, Fred Hassan, took over the pharmaceutical company when it was facing significant legal and financial problems.

"I've been facing a lot of challenges in my career. This one was the biggest I've ever seen. So I set up a roadmap as quickly as I could. I had to move forward with imperfect data, and that's where experience and insights help ... It was a very simple roadmap of five different phases ... we had to break the problem down into bite-size pieces that we could deal with, and we still had to look forward to a period when there was going to be a lot of good hope for the company. If people can see the hope—the light at the end of the tunnel—then they do build up that sense of purpose that I was trying to build ... Then also there is a sense of urgency. Once you've built up a sense of direction in terms of where you're going, you have to build up a sense of urgency. And if you can show that you can generate energy inside yourself and generate energy around you, the whole system starts to generate energy around that sense of direction, and then one gets about doing some very purposeful things."

Microsoft founder Bill Gates is famous for his energy and his drive to be the best. Interviewed in his office looking out on the huge new "Microsoft campus" in Seattle after the company had established itself as the world's leading software corporation, Gates was still hungry for more.

"We have a vision of where we are trying to go, and we're a long ways away from it ... We are not top of the networking heap, or the spreadsheet heap, or the word processing heap. Computers are not very easy to use. We don't have information at our fingertips. There is one thing that is fun—I look out there and see fun people to work with, who are learning a lot ... [But] staring out the window and saying, 'Isn't this great,' is not the solution to pushing things forward ... You've got to keep driving hard."

## In practice

- Leaders must convey their sense of burning urgency to their colleagues.

- The team needs to understand what needs to be done; the benefits of doing it and the need to do it quickly. The leader's own energy can then begin to spread through the organization.

- The sense of urgency must stay in place after the first objectives have been met. There is a real danger of allowing the organization to relax. There are always new challenges.

# 84  KEEP FIT

---

LEADERSHIP IS A stressful role. Whether you are aware of it, or not, you are almost certainly operating under an unhealthy level of stress. People react differently to stress, and most successful people have become so used to stress that they hardly notice its effects.

Take time to step back and consider what difference stress does make to your behavior, and whether you are entirely happy with that.

The most effective anti-stress programme is very simple: physical exercise.

---

## The idea

Sharon McDowell-Larsen is a senior associate and exercise physiologist with the Center for Creative Leadership and a former US Olympic Committee researcher. She recommends that we look for tell-tale signs of stress, but reminds us that we all react differently. Some people become more emotional, louder and more demanding; others retreat within themselves and become withdrawn and uncommunicative. Colleagues and family will almost certainly notice the difference more than we do.

All of these different emotional states are, in effect, abnormal; the stressed you is not the normal you.

Be wary of making significant decisions when you are stressed, especially decisions that directly concern other people.

One of the simplest ways to handle stress is to exercise. "You've heard it before, but it's true," says McDowell-Larson. "Regular exercise is the best way to stay physically healthy, and it also offers psychological benefits to counteract stress. Exercise can increase your sense of being in control, strengthen your self-esteem and help you regulate your emotions. It offers a healthy distraction from stressful situations while inducing the relaxation your body needs to dissipate its stress hormones. Regular exercise also leads to improved effectiveness as a leader. In research involving executives around the world, we've found that those who exercise regularly rate significantly higher on leadership effectiveness, as judged by their bosses, peers and direct reports, than men and women who exercise only sporadically or not at all."

## In practice

- Think about your behavior and how you behave when you are under stress. It will be different from your normal behavior and it will impact your colleagues and family.

- Whatever you do when you are stressed—which is probably to become either more aggressive or more withdrawn—realize that this is not how you would normally react, and consider the effect of that.

- Avoid making significant decisions when you are under stress, especially decisions that directly affect other people.

- Even small amounts of exercise will help. Get up from your desk and walk around. Do some minor exercises: deep breathing; arm windmills; shoulder shrugs. Close your eyes for one minute and think of nothing.

- Try to start a regime of regular exercise—perhaps with colleagues. Join the jogging club or the football team; play tennis or softball. It will do you good and encourage people to follow your example.

# 85 KNOW THE DETAIL

EFFECTIVE LEADERS KNOW their organization in detail. A good grasp of detail informs all decisions and allows leaders to ask penetrating questions and give meaningful direction to their teams.

## The idea

Alan Sugar, entrepreneur and founder of the UK electronics company Amstrad, said, "I know where every screw, nut and bolt is in my company."

Dr Ram Charan, business advisor and author, talks about the need for leaders to have a "deep immersion" in their business, especially in today's fast-moving business environment.

"I define management intensity as a deep immersion in the business's operational details and the day-to-day competitive climate the business is facing, along with hands-on involvement and follow-through. It's so important now because of the accelerating speed at which things are changing. Surviving a volatile environment requires frequent operational adjustments ... It's not enough to sit in your office and read reports and issue directives. You've got to know what's happening daily, and adjust plans and processes accordingly. Big-picture strategic thinking is still important, but it must take a back seat to this operational immersion—leaders need to be involved and visible, and communicating all the time."

Frank Zhou, general manager of pharmaceutical company Abbott International China, believes that being able to pass on detail is essential; that it is not enough to "offer some directions and then walk away".

"Many people in professional management in China are pretty young ... Some people become directors or managers at a very young age and they have not had extensive experience compared to their counterparts in Western markets. So, how can you impart discipline and professional skills to these young, ambitious and sometimes impatient people? That's the key. The way I do this is by being vigorous in terms of follow-up, in terms of details. If you just give [colleagues] a speech, or some directions, and then walk away, this may work in the US or Japan, but it may not work in China. So, in China, you have to be more determined, more focused on details, and spend more effort."

## In practice

- Few leadership actions are more impressive than demonstrating that the leader knows more about the enterprise than even an expert colleague. Leaders must understand the detail of their organization and demonstrate this to the team.

- As the speed of business change increases, leaders need to be immersed in the detail of their business in order to react quickly.

- Colleagues, especially less-experienced colleagues, need detailed instructions and follow-up to be able to perform effectively.

# 86 LEARN FROM FAILURE

NOBODY WINS ALL of the time—and the only sure way never to fail is never to take a risk, which is not an option for leaders.

The trick is to try to avoid "betting the company" on any one decision, and for the leader and the organization to learn from the inevitable failures that strew the path to success.

## The idea

John Chen, president and CEO of USA software services company Sybase Inc., says that leaders need to embrace failures: what is important is that we learn from the process.

"In some strange way you have to enjoy the negative outcome. The ball bounces both ways. Sometimes it bounces your way and sometimes it doesn't. You can only work hard enough to maximize the chances in your favor ... I think 90 percent of high achievers agree it's not just the results that are important. The path is equally, if not more, important to me. It's like playing a game. If you play a game and lose but did the best you could, you don't feel bad. Sometimes, however, you lose a game because you didn't try, and you feel really lousy. So I think the willingness to keep trying is a big part of achievement. It's actually fun to review some of the failures and what you have learned from them. It helped me tremendously. On long plane rides, I always think about the failures that hurt and what I learned from them."

Eric Schmidt, chairman and CEO of Google, says that leaders need a degree of "arrogance" to be able to believe that they can hope to instigate change, but that they must accept that there will be failures and mistakes.

"Arrogance is needed as a leadership model because you have to believe that you could actually change the world in order to attempt it, otherwise you would never try. You would just sit around and say, 'Oh woe is me'. So we temper it by the reality that we are not perfect, that we make mistakes. We've had a series of business failures, and not large ones but small ones, which we talk a lot about so we can understand the errors that we've made. So while we are not perfect, we are consensus-driven as a company. That's the reason why I spend a lot of time talking and learning from mistakes that we've made."

## In practice

- Nobody can bring about change without making mistakes and experiencing failures.

- Sometimes even your best efforts will not be rewarded with success.

- Failures are a huge resource of valuable information: learn from failures; ensure that the organization has learned the same lessons; move on.

# 87 | MANAGE YOUR TIME

MANAGING OUR TIME is the single most important thing that we can do to improve our effectiveness, but most of us are really bad at it.

## The idea

Naj Al-Awadhi is deputy CEO of Dubai Media and the youngest member of the United Arab Emirates parliament. She has quickly risen to significant leadership roles in what is still a male-dominated society. She believes in focusing on the real priorities, after which everything else is just a question of time management.

"It is critical to balance everything and unhealthy not to. I believe in defining in your heart and mind what is important in your life and what will still be important in your life 40 years from now, and then prioritizing based on that. After you have done that, the rest is all about solid time and task management."

Business and management thinker, Peter Drucker, points out that to get things done, leaders need substantial chunks of time available. "To be effective," he says, "every executive ... needs to be able to dispose of time in fairly large chunks. To have small dribs and drabs of time at his disposal will not be sufficient even if the total is an impressive number of hours. This is particularly true with respect to time spent working with people."

Drucker's recommendations are: cut out the things that need not be done at all. "Ask yourself the question: 'What would happen if this were not done at all?' And if the answer is, 'Nothing would happen', then obviously the conclusion is to stop doing it ... The next question is: 'Which of these activities on my time log could be done by somebody else just as well, if not better?'" Finally, leaders should ask themselves if they are themselves wasting other people's time to no purpose. "Effective executives have learned to ask systematically and without coyness: 'What do I do that wastes your time without contributing to your effectiveness?'"

Drucker lists time-wasting factors in the organization as "the recurring crisis"—a regular occurrence that the organization has not learnt to deal with systematically—and "malorganization", whose key symptom is "an excess of meetings". He also argues that overstaffing can lead to time-wasting. "People get in each other's way ... In a lean organization, people have room to move without colliding with one another and can do their work without having to explain it all the time."

## In practice

- Set key priorities and manage your time around them.

- Analyze how you spend your time: cut out things that don't need doing at all, things that other people could do and time that you spend with other people that is not productive.

- Look for faults in the organization that are wasting people's time: lack of system and foresight; too many meetings; possibly even too many people.

- Consolidate your newly free time into useable chunks.

# QUICK WINS

---

MAKING A FEW quick fixes helps to establish a new leader's credentials. However, the search for quick wins should not be obsessive, and it should not be at the expense of colleagues. Most quick wins should be a collective effort.

---

## The idea

When Alan Leighton became chairman of the UK's Royal Mail, the national postal service had recently been renamed Consignia as part of management changes that had attempted to revitalize the organization. The changes had not worked, and the Consignia name—which was widely disliked—was also associated with failure. Leighton changed the name back to the "Royal Mail" (with quick royal permission gained via Charles, Prince of Wales, with whom Leighton had worked in connection with the Prince's Trust, a charity aimed at creating opportunities for young people).

"The Royal Mail was all about its heritage," said Leighton, "which was royal and British, a fact reflected in its uniform and red livery. The core idea was that it was much more than just a company. I knew it would also give me a quick win on taking the chair to reverse the unpopular change and ditch the Consignia name for good; and a quick win is very useful for any new boy. It would help to prove to critics, fed up with lacklustre service, that we really meant business."

On the other hand, Mark E. Van Buren and Todd Safferstone of The Corporate Executive Board Company have written about the "Quick Wins Paradox". Their research demonstrated that an excessive focus on quick wins can lead to insensitive behavior that damages leaders' relationships with their new teams.

As a Harvard Business Review article by the authors reports, "In a study of more than 5,400 new leaders, the authors found that struggling leaders tended to exhibit five behaviors characteristic of people overly intent on securing a quick win. They focused too much on details, reacted negatively to criticism, intimidated others, jumped to conclusions, and micromanaged their direct reports. Some managed to eke out a win anyway, but the fallout was often toxic. The leaders who were thriving in their new roles, by contrast, shared not only a strong focus on results—necessary for early successes—but also excellent change-management skills. They communicated a clear vision, developed constructive relationships, and built team capabilities ... Collective quick wins established credibility and prepared them to lead their teams to harder-won victories."

## In practice

- Early quick wins are valuable for any leader. They establish your presence and prove that you have the ability to make things happen. They can impress the organization and the outside world.

- The search for quick wins should not become obsessive and it must not be achieved by railroading changes past your new colleagues.

- Establishing good team relationships and achieving collective quick wins early on will set the scene for the concerted team effort that will be required to tackle more fundamental problems.

# 89 RECOGNIZE PEOPLE

NOTHING BINDS PEOPLE to a leader more effectively than a personal connection; a proof that the leader recognizes individuals and values their input.

Leaders should try to get to know as many of their team as possible. Being recognized and addressed by name makes people feel valued and appreciated.

## The idea

The great French general, Napoleon Bonaparte, later to become Emperor of France, inspired fanatical loyalty from his army. He was quick to reward conspicuous acts of bravery and feats of arms, often making immediate promotions and awards on the battlefield itself. It was said that he never forgot a face, and that he was often able to remember names, and even to recall on which campaign a soldier had served with him. Napoleon worked hard at this ability, however, spending time committing lists of names to his prodigious memory.

The memoirs of Madame de Rémusat, lady-in-waiting to Napoleon's wife, the Empress Josephine, provide a vivid contemporary account of Napoleon as seen through the eyes of the imperial court.

"Bonaparte's reception by the troops was nothing short of rapturous. It was well worth seeing how he talked to the soldiers, how he questioned them one after the other respecting their campaigns or their wounds, taking particular interest in the men who had accompanied him to Egypt. I have heard Madame Bonaparte say that her husband was in the constant habit of poring over the list of what are called the cadres of the army at night before he slept.

He would go to sleep repeating the names of the corps, and even those of some of the individuals who composed them; he kept these names in a corner of his memory, and this habit came to his aid when he wanted to recognize a soldier and to give him the pleasure of a cheering word from his general. He spoke to the subalterns in a tone of good-fellowship, which delighted them all, as he reminded them of their common feats of arms."

## In practice

- Being able to recognize members of the extended team is a great asset for any leader. It makes people feel valued and it binds them to the leader.

- There is no substitute for genuine recognition: being able to remember that you have met a person before, and in what part of the organization they work, is a start; being able to put a name to the face is best.

- This is not easy to do, even in a medium-sized organization: time spent studying staff lists would be rewarded.

- Ask colleagues to brief you about colleagues you are about to meet to help refresh your memory.

# REINVENT YOURSELF

If you think that a new and more radical strategy is needed, consider "reinventing" yourself and your team.

## The idea

After Andrea Jung had already been chairman and CEO of Avon Products Inc. for many years, she realized that the strategies for which she was responsible were not succeeding.

"If you need an example of what is meant by the courage of leadership, this was it. There was a moment when I had to have the humility to undo my own strategies; undo my own team." Her mentor advised her to go home that night and pretend that she had been fired, and then to come in the next morning and imagine that she was an outsider, hired to make fast, tough and objective decisions to save the company. "It was probably some of the most pivotal advice that I have ever received. I came back in the next morning and we did some bold things in terms of radical organizational restructuring. With emotional detachment from existing strategies we made some very tough decisions, and it really breathed a very important new chapter of life into the company."

Wu Xiaobing, president and managing director of pharmaceutical company Wyeth China, uses a similar approach with the whole management team.

During a brainstorm session in which colleagues are encouraged to criticize past decisions, he asks: "If every member of our management team left the company for whatever reasons ... what would a new management team do? Would they be content with the growth rate

... that we've had over the past years? Or would they want to grow even faster, to show they are more capable? If so, then they have to learn two things. First, what did their predecessors do wrong, or not well enough? Secondly, going forward, what will be the important opportunities? So, everyone has to forget his identity and imagine he is a new team member; it doesn't matter what has happened in the past, you can criticize the company fiercely. And indeed, after our brainstorming and discussion, we have been surprised that we had a lot of conclusions and there are many things we haven't done well."

## In practice

- If your strategy isn't working, step back and consider a whole new approach.

- Imagine that you are a new leader facing the current situation for the first time; view the current situation objectively and consider more radical solutions.

- Take action as if you were that new leader. Put aside your involvement with previous strategies and approaches.

- The team members already trust you and are loyal to you, so your new direction will be easier for them to embrace than if it was proposed by an outsider.

- Asking colleagues to imagine themselves as a fresh new team assessing the organization's past performance helps the team to examine its own performance critically but positively.

# 91 SAY NO TO DISTRACTIONS

LEADERS ARE SOUGHT after by local communities, lobbyists, political parties and charities, as governors, directors, advisors and cheerleaders. Too many commitments can be exhausting; saying "no" can be a liberating experience.

## The idea

Jacob Wallenberg is chairman of Investor AB, a Swedish investment company founded in 1916 as the investment wing of Stockholm's Enskilda Bank, which was founded in the 19th century by an one of Jacob's ancestors. The illustrious Wallenberg family includes bankers, industrialists, politicians and diplomats.

"My grandfather and father worked seven days a week. To them, there was no difference between private life and professional life. They never stopped working, and that was what I saw as I grew up." Wallenberg believes that this culture has changed. Speaking personally, he finds the need to create space in which to think. "If I compare myself to most people around me, I work hard, but I've also tried to draw some kind of line between the roles ... you have to find a way of stopping the world for a second so that you can reflect and think. You can't just perform the whole time. I find myself not reflecting enough, but because of the responsibility of my job I have to find a way to make this a priority. It is a challenge to find an intelligent way of dealing with that in this day and age. For example, I've declined to take board positions in order to give myself more time. I spend time talking to people about the big picture and I travel a fair bit, which is an excellent way to gain perspective on things."

Brenda Barnes decided to take a career break from her role as president of PepsiCo North America in order to bring up her three children. She then returned to work as CEO of USA consumer goods company, Sara Lee. She talks about managing her time and how she became more able to say "no" to distractions to her key priorities: her work and her family.

"Time. Time. Balance to me, that's all it is, time. You can do both, you just can't do anything else. Everything else has to go, including sleep ... After I had children I became a better time manager. I was more disciplined in how I spent my time. I also got comfortable saying, 'I'm not doing that, I'm not doing that,' and not thinking about it."

## In practice

- Leaders have limited resources of time and energy. They also need to be able to step back from the daily workload and reflect.

- Find time for thought and reflection.

- Make your family or social life a priority.

- There are demands on your time and energy from outside work. Do what you feel strongly about, but be ruthless in saying no to distractions.

# THINK LATERALLY

LEADERS NEED CONSTANTLY to challenge perceived wisdom; they need to think about whether there is a different and better way of doing things, and they need to encourage the whole organization to think in this way. Unfortunately, our brains are programmed to assume that the future will be like the past.

## The idea

Frans Johansson, author of *The Medici Effect*, writes about our inbuilt tendency to assume that the future will be like the past. Our minds (for very practical reasons) tend to create what Johansson calls "associative barriers". Any one idea sets off an associative chain of other ideas that we are familiar with: we jump to conclusions.

"We are more likely to make assumptions ... than maintain a mind that is open to all possibilities ... The effect is subtle, but very powerful ... By simply hearing a word or seeing an image, the mind unlocks a whole string of associated ideas, each one connecting to another." These chains of association are efficient—they help us to assess situations quickly and to take appropriate action—but they also carry costs. "They inhibit our ability to think broadly. We do not question assumptions as readily; we jump to conclusions faster and create barriers to alternate ways of thinking about a particular situation."

Johansson suggests some techniques that can help to break down these automatic assumptions and to help to see all of the possibilities in any given situation. One way of trying to break away from familiar associations is to explore "reverse" scenarios: maybe a restaurant should have no menus, not charge money for food or not serve food at all. (Perhaps the chef creates individual dishes to order from the ingredients that he has that day; perhaps food is free, but people pay for time spent in the restaurant; perhaps people bring their own food but pay for the location.)

This process does not necessarily result in a workable new idea, but it makes us challenge our pre-conceptions about what a restaurant should be. Similarly, Johansson suggests that we make a reverse assumption and then think how to make it happen: high street banks want to attract customers; assume that they do not; what should they do actively to drive customers away?

## In practice

- We all tend to make unconscious chains of association, on the assumption that what has worked in the past will work in the future.

- Question assumptions and received wisdom and keep an open mind. Challenge colleagues to try and see things differently and to imagine radical new scenarios.

- Some mental exercises, like reverse thinking, can help us to break out of entrenched ways of seeing things.

# PART 8
# YOU AND THE
# OUTSIDE WORLD

# 93 ASSUME THE WORST

---

WHEN DEALING WITH a crisis that brings an apparent failure of the organization into the public arena, assume the worst. There is a tendency to be overly optimistic and to assume that things will turn out well. There is also a tendency to forget that news media need drama and crisis, and that a problem will be portrayed in its most lurid and negative light.

---

## The idea

In the 1980s, America's General Electric Company (GE) faced an apparently minor issue: it was alleged that some workers at a GE plant producing military components for the US Government were claiming for time that they had not worked. GE investigations suggested that the fraud was on a very minor scale, and that over 99% of time-cards at the plant were fairly and accurately completed. However, Caspar Weinberger, recently appointed as Secretary of Defense by President Ronald Reagan, raised the issue in support of his campaign against "fraud, waste and abuse" in military expenditure.

In his 1980 presidential campaign Reagan had promised a significant increase in military expenditure, whilst also promising smaller and more efficient federal government; there was a drive to "obtain the best value for our defense dollars". The affair of the fraudulent GE timesheets became a major issue played out in the national media.

Jack Welch, chairman and CEO of General Electric from 1981 to 2001, faced this crisis early in his career. His advice to leaders, based on his experience, is to assume the following:

1.   The problem is worse than it appears

2. Everyone will eventually find out everything

3. You and your organization's handling of the crisis will be portrayed in the worst possible light

4. Changes in process will have to be put in place and there will probably be personnel changes

5. The organization will survive, and in the long term will be stronger for having ridden out the crisis

Dr Ram Charan, business advisor and author, confirms that leaders tend not to assume the worst. "Actually, in a crisis most leaders tend to be too optimistic rather than the contrary. They overestimate how well their company will fare because they want to believe everything will turn out well. This misplaced optimism allows them to think that they don't have to make painful decisions or take drastic action. To guard against this, I advise all leaders to map out worst-case scenarios. If you deliberately plan for the worst, you'll probably encounter something less dire and come out ahead when it's over."

## In practice

- If an internal issue has the potential to interest the media, assume that everything that can be discovered will be discovered and then portrayed in the worst possible light.

- Take firm, decisive and, if necessary, drastic action. If a colleague has been negligent or worse, they cannot and should not be protected.

- The organization will survive, and will eventually emerge strengthened by the experience.

- Planning for worst-case scenarios can help leaders to be prepared for a sudden crisis.

# 94  ATTRACT AND ENCOURAGE TALENT

THE LIMITING ASSET of the 21$^{st}$ century may well be talent. Leaders must work hard to attract young talent, ensuring that their organization has a reputation as a place where people want to work and where there is a commitment to developing people.

## The idea

Ruben Vardanian, chairman and CEO of Russia's oldest private investment bank, believes that the availability of skilled and talented people will be the defining issue for businesses in the current century.

"The question for leaders is how we can create a system to attract the best people, because the main fight of the 21$^{st}$ century is not about assets. The main struggle in the 19$^{th}$ century was about land. In the 20$^{th}$ century, it was about industrial assets and natural resources. In 21$^{st}$ century, the main fight will be for the best people. Because people need to believe they want to work for you, that they can realize themselves in your company. To attract them, we need to have the right system in place and develop them for the long-term. Many companies are not ready to do this because they hire people, but they don't spend enough time or effort in developing them. I think leaders need to be very, very committed to these types of things."

Azim Premji, chairman of Wipro, India's largest software company, highlights the need to spread the net of recruitment as widely as possible.

"For one thing, we have spread our recruitment net wider than the top five business schools in India; we now hire people from the top 25 management institutes. We have MBAs whom we have recruited from these institutes, and they rank very close in quality to people we hire from the IIMs [Indian Institutes of Management] ... In fact, last year we took in 160 people from these schools. Second, we do lots of internal training and give people major responsibilities even if they are only 60% ready. Our experience is that people are pretty elastic when you give them responsibility, and they just grow rapidly with the job."

Some successful business people have chosen to fund colleges that will supply the talented young people of the future. UK businessman Phillip Green, owner of several of the UK's largest retail operations, helped to finance the UK Fashion Retail Academy, motivated by his problems in filling vacancies at his Arcadia clothing empire.

James Dyson, industrial designer and entrepreneur, founded the Dyson School for Design and Innovation to encourage Britain's next generation of designers and inventors.

## In practice

- The ability to find, attract and retain talented and skilled people may be the defining issue of 21$^{st}$ century business.

- Recruiting talent is only the first step; people must be encouraged, developed, trained and stretched.

- Organizations should develop close links with the relevant educational establishments. If these do not exist, it may be necessary to help to create them.

# 95 BE ACCOUNTABLE

A LEADER HAS TO accept responsibility for the actions of their team. In difficult circumstances, stakeholders in the company and the general public will expect to see the leader, in person, addressing issues directly and demonstrating clear accountability.

## The idea

When American car giant Chrysler encountered financial difficulties in the 1980s, its recovery was led by Lee Iacocca, who led a drastic programme of restructuring and cost-cutting, selling the company's loss-making European operation to Peugeot.

He also revitalized Chrysler's product line and, critically, successfully lobbied the United States Congress to guarantee loans that would enable the company to stay afloat. The first press advertisements attempted to win over public and government opinion for the loan guarantee scheme, under the headline *"Would America be better off without Chrysler?"* The ads carried Iacocca's signature.

Iacocca said, "We wanted to show the public that a new era had begun. After all, a chief executive of a company that's going broke has to reassure people. He has to say: 'I'm here, I'm real, and I'm responsible for this company. And to show that I mean it, I'm signing on the dotted line'. At long last, we would be able to convey that there was some genuine accountability at Chrysler. By putting my signature on these ads, we were inviting the public to write to me with their complaints and their questions. We were announcing that this large, complex company was now being run by a human being who was putting his name and his reputation on the line."

As the company's finances began to recover, Iacocca launched a consumer advertising campaign in which he himself appeared, promoting his company's products. Using the slogan *"The pride is back"*, the advertisements also featured what was to become Iacocca's trademark catch phrase: *"If you can find a better car, buy it."* Consumer confidence in Chrysler rapidly recovered.

## In practice

- A leader is accountable for everything that happens in the organization. When things go wrong, the leader must be seen to be accountable, and to be available to the public via the media.

- Organizations where no leader can be identified as responsible are seen as being rudderless and without direction. There is no alternative to accountability.

- When leaders succeed in identifying themselves with an organization, consumers and stakeholders are reassured to see that there is a visible figurehead; a person who has made himself or herself accountable for the whole organization.

# 96  DO THE RIGHT THING

ORGANIZATIONS MUST OPERATE ethically. Companies that exploit their employees or the environment, or that fail to work successfully with their local or global communities, will increasingly find themselves subject to damaging criticism. They will also find it very hard to recruit and retain talent.

## The idea

Sir Christopher Gent, chairman of GlaxoSmithKline, says that trust is an organization's "licence to trade".

"The need to be valued in your community is becoming more of an issue. There has to be a level of trust, because that trust is your licence to trade. It's absolutely critical in a pharmaceutical business such as GlaxoSmithKline. After all, it's a matter of life or death for the people we care for. This perception of community value is now pretty widely accepted."

Indra Nooyi, chairman and CEO of PepsiCo, talks of the moral need to respect the environment, and about the need for companies to demonstrate ethical and sustainable practices.

"We call this 'performance with purpose', and environment sustainability is a critical part of that performance with purpose. Basically, our goal is to make sure that when it comes to water and energy, we replenish the environment and leave it in a net zero state. So across the world we have unleashed the power of our people to come up with ideas to reduce, recycle, replenish the environment— and we are making great progress by reducing how much water we use in our manufacture and the carbon footprint that we put on the environment. As a consequence, what we are seeing is an incredible investment in all these environment initiatives ... really in two ways: one is tangible financial investment; second is a huge return on investment and because new employees are usually idealistic young people who just graduated from college. They want to come to a company to work for a purpose, that is wise about the next generation. And they see PepsiCo really making a difference to an environment as a whole. They really want to work at PepsiCo because they want a company that is working on meaning rather than just taking."

## In practice

- Being in business means making ethical decisions. There is a moral imperative to behave well towards the environment, the local and national communities and employees. There is also a practical imperative: organizations that behave badly may lose the "licence to trade" offered by the trust of the community in which they do business.

- People buy brands that they trust. In the modern world, "trust" has a wide context that goes beyond trusting the brand to deliver its immediate promises and includes a wide range of ethical behaviors.

- Talented people will increasingly want to work for organizations that they believe are making a positive contribution to local and global concerns and which operate in an ethical way.

# 97 | LEAD FOR YOUR INDUSTRY

SOME IMPORTANT THINGS that affect your company are apparently beyond your control: they are driven by government or regulatory bodies and affect the whole industry. A leader can decide to lead for the industry.

## The idea

Peter Martin is chief operating officer of Norgine, a privately owned pharmaceutical company. Several of the company's most important products are "branded generic" products—specially reformulated versions of generically available drugs.

When Norgine's own representative industry body, the Association of the British Pharmaceutical Industry (ABPI), proposed a cost-saving measure to the British government that would introduce the automatic substitution by pharmacists of the cheapest generic drug available, even when the patient's doctor had prescribed a specific brand, Martin felt that the ABPI were no longer representing the best interests of his company, or of other pharmaceutical companies of a similar size. He also believed passionately that the new legislation was not in the long-term interest of the industry, nor of patients, and would not necessarily result in cost savings.

"My favorite quotation is that line of George Bernard Shaw's," says Martin. "'The reasonable man adapts himself to the world; the unreasonable one persists in trying to adapt the world to himself. Therefore all progress depends on the unreasonable man.' I decided that I had to be that unreasonable man."

Norgine, led by Peter Martin and with the full support of his chairman, dramatically resigned from their industry body, the ABPI. Martin began to network with a group of like-minded other companies and hired a PR firm to run the campaign to lobby government. A petition was launched, asking the British prime minister to hold a public consultation on the issue. Martin worked closely with the pharmaceutical industry's trade press to get an airing for the company's position and his company funded nearly all of the costs of the campaign, preferring to spearhead the campaign rather than to create a more cumbersome cross-industry committee.

In January 2010, the UK's Department of Health announced that it would hold the desired public consultation.

## In practice

- Decisions by government, or other regulatory and legislative bodies, appear to be beyond your control.

- Leaders can decide to challenge these decisions and to lead for their industry sector.

- Your own organization may or may not be the main beneficiary of success, but if nobody else will do it—do it yourself. Ensure that you have the support of your board.

- Network, lobby and work the media. Bring the rest of the industry with you.

# 98  LOOK FOR PARTNERSHIPS

EVERY ORGANIZATION IS dependent on a complex network of relationships that enable it to do business. Some of these relationships could be turned into significant partnerships.

## The idea

After founding Apple in 1976 with Steve Wozniac and taking the company public in 1980, Steve Jobs was removed from managerial duties in a boardroom power struggle in 1985 and resigned from the company that he had created. Twelve years later, when Jobs' subsequent venture was bought by Apple, Jobs re-emerged as Apple's CEO.

One of his first actions was to arrange a strategic partnership with the software giant Microsoft, with whom Apple had been engaged in a drawn-out and costly series of legal arguments over patent rights. In 1997 Steve Jobs took to the stage to deliver one of his famous keynote speeches.

"Now, I'd like to talk about meaningful partnerships. Apple lives in an ecosystem and it needs help from other partners; it needs to help other partners. And relationships that are destructive don't help anybody in this industry as it is today. So during the last several weeks we have looked at some of the relationships, and one has stood out as a relationship that hasn't been going so well, but that has the potential, I think, to be great for both companies. And I'd like to announce one of our first partnerships today; a very, very meaningful one. And that is one with Microsoft ... We have to let go of this notion that for Apple to win, Microsoft has to lose ... the era of setting this up as a competition between Apple and Microsoft is over as far as I'm concerned. This is about getting Apple healthy and ... about Apple being able to make incredibly great contributions to the computer industry, to be healthy and prosper again."

In the same market, Louis Gerstner of IBM decided that IBM should move out of software development and "stop deluding ourselves about our proficiency in this part of the stack". Instead, he sent out the message that IBM wanted to work with the leading software developers.

"What we said to them was: 'We are going to leave this market to you; we are going to be your partner rather than your competitor; we will work with you to make sure your applications run superbly on our hardware, and we will support your applications with our services group'. And rather than just have lunch with them and saying 'let's be partners', we structured detailed commitments, revenue and share targets, and measurements by which both parties agreed to abide."

## In practice

- There are many possible useful partnerships with organizations who share a common interest: the same facilities; a similar market; the same supply chain.

- Think laterally about the organizations that could potentially benefit your organization in the longer term; these might include educational establishments, consumer groupings, museums and exhibitions.

- Think big. Look for a major partnership that could enable you to face the market more powerfully together than you do in your current relationship.

- Consider letting some things go; perhaps a new partner could deliver some aspect of your current service better than you do.

- When you make a new partnership, be specific; set out commitments, targets and measurements.

# MAKE A CONTRIBUTION

ORGANIZATIONS EXIST TO make a contribution to society: to bring talent, ideas and capital together in order to achieve something.

## The idea

David Packard, co-founder of Hewlett-Packard, was one of the earliest industrialists to make the point that an organization's fundamental purpose is to make a contribution.

"I think many people assume, wrongly, that a company exists simply to make money. While this is an important result of a company's existence, we have to go deeper and find the real reasons for our being ... A group of people get together and exist as an institution ... so that they are able to accomplish something collectively which they could not accomplish separately. They are able to do something worthwhile—they make a contribution to society."

Companies also increasingly make contributions through their charitable donations and strategic involvements with community projects. Timberland Boot Company's charitable commitment to City Year, a non-profit organization that brings together young people of all backgrounds for a year of full-time community service, began to turn into a more significant partnership when company executives met with the co-founder of City Year.

"The meeting was important," says Timberland marketing vice-president Ken Freitas, "because for the first time we realized that there was more here than a typical charitable contribution. There was a real connection. The similarities between what each organization wanted to do and how it planned to achieve its vision were striking."

The two organizations developed an ongoing partnership, with Timberland sponsoring City Year events and Timberland employees volunteering for City Year projects. Employees take great pride in this partnership with City Year, and feel that both they and the organization are making a positive contribution to society.

Muhammad Yunus, the founder of Grameen Bank, pioneered a new kind of community banking, offering very small loans to small enterprises in Bangladesh without requiring collateral security. Each borrower must belong to a group of five other borrowers, creating peer pressure on individual members not to let down the group as a whole by defaulting.

The great majority of borrowers are women, and default rates are lower than for traditional banking systems. The small loans have helped thousands of small enterprises to establish themselves in poor rural areas. Yunus identifies people whose main concern in life will be to make a contribution to society and who may choose to work in non-profit organizations as a result.

"They are totally committed to make a difference to the world. They are social-objective driven. They want to give a better chance in life to other people. They want to achieve their objective through creating/supporting sustainable business enterprises. Their businesses may or may not earn profit, but like any other businesses they must not incur losses. They create a new class of business which we may describe as 'non-loss' business."

## In practice

- Companies must make a profit in order to justify the capital that they use, and to prove their success and efficiency, but the fundamental purpose of any company is to make a contribution.

- Companies are increasingly using their profits to make a further contribution to society through charitable donations.

- These charitable activities can develop into significant strategic partnerships involving both organizations at many levels. Employees can gain great satisfaction from knowing that their company is contributing to communities though such partnerships and are likely to become personally involved.

- Talented young people will increasingly choose to work for organizations that can demonstrate that they are making a contribution.

# SEE THE
# BIGGER PICTURE

ONE SIGNIFICANT CHARACTERISTIC of really successful leaders is their ability to see the bigger picture. A leader who can successfully predict significant movements of markets or of society as a whole is at a huge advantage.

The other sense of "seeing the bigger picture" is to see one's organization from the broadest possible perspective, in terms of its relationship with employees, stakeholders and with society as a whole.

## The idea

Bill Gates, ex-CEO of Microsoft, was one of the first people in the world to see that computers might become a universal household product. A fellow undergraduate at Harvard University remembers:

"Bill was one of the first people I ever knew who really had this concept of computers being everywhere ... He saw that as being the future ... He also talked to me about the concept of everyone being able to discard all the books and paper materials and access everything they wanted to know by computer—to do all communication by computers."

The student also recalls that Gates imagined personal computers would be omnipresent in people's homes, but not in offices.

Harvard Business School professor and author Michael Beer made a study of the leaders of what he calls "High Commitment High Performance" organizations; companies that had held a position in the top half of their industry for 10 years or more, and within which what Beer calls a "high commitment" culture had been created.

"The CEOs were quite different in personality, background, and leadership style. But they were similar in what they saw as the purpose of the firm. They shared the view that a firm has a larger purpose than simply profit and increasing stock price, although they were all laser-focused on profitability and saw it as essential to achieving their larger purpose for the firm. They had a multi-stakeholder view of the firm as opposed to a shareholder view. The purpose was to add value to employees, customers, community, and society—not just shareholders. These CEOs operate from deep beliefs and values. Their purpose is to leave a legacy of a great firm."

## In practice

- Leaders who see the bigger picture in terms of movements of markets and of society as a whole have a huge advantage over the competition.

- The most successful corporate leaders have a habit of seeing the organization as a whole; taking into consideration employees, consumers and every other stakeholder, as well as shareholders.

- These leaders consider the organization's relationship with society and are concerned with the larger purpose of the organization.

# SOURCES

1.  **Mission, Vision, Values, Change**

**Have a vision**

Sam Walton: http://walmartstores.com/AboutUs/8123.aspx

Wu Xiaobing: http://www.knowledgeatwharton.com.cn/index.cfm?fa=viewArticle
&articleID=1968

**Establish your mission**

Jack Welch: Jack Welch, *Winning*, Harper Collins, London 2005, pp14–15.

John Mackey: http://marketplace.publicradio.org/segments/corneroffice/corner_
mackey_transcript.html

**Establish your values**

Colleen Barrett: http://www.knowledgeatwharton.com.cn/index.cfm?fa=viewArtic
le&articleID=1882

Dieter Zetsche: http://www.knowledgeatwharton.com.cn/index.cfm?fa=viewArtic
le&articleID=1810

Subroto Bagchi: S. Balasubramanian, *The Art of Business Leadership*, Response
Books, New Delhi, 2007, pp 224–225

**Make it happen**

Michael Eisner: http://marketplace.publicradio.org/display/web/2009/08/13/pm-
corner-office-eisner-transcript

Louis Gerstner: Louis Gerstner, *Who says elephants can't dance?* Harper Collins,
New York, 2002, pp 229–230

**Seek out change**

John Kotter: *A Force for Change*, The Free Press, Macmillan Inc, NY, 1990, p 35

Sir Richard Branson: Richard Branson, *Business Stripped Bare*, Virgin Books, London, 2008, p III; p 192


## 2. You and the Top Team

**Build the perfect top team**

Daisy Poon: http://www.knowledgeatwharton.com.cn/index.cfm?fa=viewArticle&articleID=2023

**Challenge the management structure**

Nick Yang: http://meetinnovators.com/2009/10/08/nick-yang-from-kongzhong-corporation

Zhang Ruimin: http://www.knowledgeatwharton.com.cn/index.cfm?fa=viewArticle&articleID=2060

**Collaborate**

Bill George: http://www.billgeorge.org/page/the-new-leaders-collaborative-not-commanding

Marten Hansen: http://www.thecollaborationbook.com/hansen.pdf

**Delegate**

Lee Iacocca: Lee Iacocca, *Iacocca, An Autobiography*, Sedgwick & Jackson, London 1985, p 56

Sir John Harvey-Jones: John Harvey-Jones, *Making it Happen: Reflections on Leadership*, William Collins, London, 1988, p 50

**Devolve decision making**

Irene Rosenfeld: http://marketplace.publicradio.org/display/web/2009/02/10/corneroffice_rosenfeld_transcript/

John Mackey: http://www.fastcompany.com/magazine/84/wholefoods.
html?page=0%2C0

## Leader-managers

John Kotter: John P. Kotter, *A Force for Change*, The Free Press, Macmillan Inc,
NY, 1990, p 17, pp 62–63

## Make the budget work

Jack Welch: Jack Welch, *Winning*, Harper Collins, London 2005, pp 197–198

Nancy Snyder: http://www.businessweek.com/innovate/content/mar2006/
id20060306_287425.htm

## Plan for your succession

John Birt Baron Birt/Greg Dyke: Greg Dyke, *Inside Story*, Harper Collins, London,
2004, p 145

Rebekah Wade: Alan Leighton, *On Leadership*, Random House Business Books,
London, 2007, p 225

## 3.  You and the Whole Team

## Allow choice to drive decisions

Mukesh Ambani: http://www.rediff.com/money/2007/jan/17inter.htm

## Be clear

Mike Southon and Chris West: Mike Southon, Chris West, *The Boardroom
Entrepreneur*, Random House, London, 2005, p 72

Bryan Huang: Juan Antonio Fernandez, Laurie Underwood *China CEO*, John
Wiley & Sons (Asia) Pte Ltd, Singapore, 2006, p 83

Seiichi Kawasaki: ibid, p 85

## Be demanding

Comments on Bill Gates: James Wallace, Jim Erickson, *Hard Drive*, John Wiley & Sons, New York, 1992, pp 128–129

## Be fair

Jonah Lehrer: Jonah Lehrer, *The decisive moment*, Canongate Books Ltd, Edinburgh, 2009, pp 175–176

David Packard: Speech by Dave Packard to HP managers March 8, 1960, quoted in David Packard, *The HP Way*, Harper Collins, New York, 1995, p xxvii

Sir John Harvey-Jones: John Harvey-Jones, *Making it Happen: Reflections on Leadership*, William Collins, London, 1988, pp 68–69

## Communicate all of the time

Carly Fiorina: *Tough Choices*, Nicholas Brealey, Boston, 2006, p 203

John Kotter: John P. Kotter, *A Force for Change,* The Free Press, Macmillan Inc, NY, 1990, p 50

Martha Lane Fox: Alan Leighton, *On Leadership*, Random House Business Books, London, 2007, p 20

## Communicate in crisis

Andrea Jung: http://www.egonzehnder.com/global/focus/archive/id/99302140

Gerard Kleisterlee: http://www.egonzehnder.com/global/focus/leadersdialogue/article/id/71500010

## Communicate simply

President John F. Kennedy: Presidential nomination acceptance speech 15 July 1960

## Communicate the vision

Bob Iger: http://marketplace.publicradio.org/segments/corneroffice/corner_iger_transcript.html

John Ryan: http://www.forbes.com/2009/12/30/chief-listening-officer-leadership-managing-ccl.html

**Create action groups**

Alan Leighton: Alan Leighton, *On Leadership*, Random House Business Books, London, 2007, pp 228–229

Mike Southon and Chris West: Mike Southon, Chris West, *The Boardroom Entrepreneur*, Random House, London, 2005, pp 41–61

**Create followers**

Anne Mulcahy: http://www.nytimes.com/2009/03/22/business/22corner.html?pagewanted=3

W. L. Gore & Associates: Gary Hamel, *The Future of Management*, Harvard Business School Publishing, Boston MA, USA, 2007, pp 91–93

**Distance and closeness**

Rob Goffee and Gareth Jones: http://hbswk.hbs.edu/archive/5199.html

**Don't get complacent**

Stuart Rose: http://www.guardian.co.uk/business/2004/jun/05/marksspencer

Sir Richard Branson: Richard Branson, *Business Stripped Bare*, Virgin Books, London, 2008, pp 261–262

**Encourage candor**

Jack Welch: Jack Welch, *Winning*, Harper Collins, London 2005, p27; p 32

Jun Tang: Juan Antonio Fernandez, Laurie Underwood *China CEO*, John Wiley & Sons (Asia) Pte Ltd, Singapore, 2006, p 84

**Encourage real debate**

Dieter Zetsche: http://www.knowledgeatwharton.com.cn/index.cfm?fa=viewArticle&articleID=1810

Alan Mulally: http://marketplace.publicradio.org/display/web/2008/01/15/corner_
office_mulally_transcript

**Engage people's emotions**

Robert McKee: http://hbswk.hbs.edu/archive/3583.html

Greg Dyke: Greg Dyke, *Inside Story*, Harper Collins, London, 2004, p 214–215

**Get feedback**

Anne Mulcahy: http://www.nytimes.com/2009/03/22/business/22corner.
html?pagewanted=2

Archie Norman: Alan Leighton, *On Leadership*, Random House Business Books,
London, 2007, p 68

**Get people aligned**

John Kotter: John P. Kotter, *A Force for Change*, The Free Press, Macmillan Inc,
NY, 1990, p 5, p 49

Michael Beer & Nitin Nohria: http://hbswk.hbs.edu/item/2166.html

**Give people autonomy**

Harsh Mariwala: S. Balasubramanian, *The Art of Business Leadership*, Response
Books, New Delhi, 2007, p 210

William Weldon: http://www.knowledgeatwharton.com.cn/index.cfm?fa=viewArt
icle&articleID=1862

Reynold Levy: http://marketplace.publicradio.org/display/web/2007/10/25/corner_
office_levy_transcript/

**Give the team the tools to do the job**

Fred Smith: http://marketplace.publicradio.org/display/web/2009/03/11/pm_
corneroffice_fedex_smith_transcript

Marshall Goldsmith, *What got you here won't get you there*, Profile Books, London, 2008, p 69

## Involve the team

Vice-Admiral the Viscount Nelson: Robert Southey, *The Life of Nelson*, Kessinger Publishing, 2005, p 127

Dhirubhai Ambani: http://www.rediff.com/money/2007/jan/17inter.htm

## Make it fun

Dan Nye: http://www.forbes.com/2007/04/20/linkedin-social-networking-lead-careers-cx_tw_0420facetime.html?partner=leadership_newsletter

Jacqueline Novogratz: https://www.mckinseyquarterly.com/ghost.aspx?ID=/Women_and_leadership_Learning_from_the_social_sector_2336

## Options and consensus

Sir John Harvey-Jones: John Harvey-Jones, *Making it Happen: Reflections on Leadership*, William Collins, London, 1988, pp 75–76

The Toyota Way: http://www.si.umich.edu/ICOS/Liker04.pdf

## Transform the team

James MacGregor Burns, *Leadership*, Harper Perennial Modern Classics, New York, 2010

Jarvis Snook: http://www.hrmagazine.co.uk/news/985910/Interview-Jarvis-Snook-CEO-Rok/

## Trust your employees

Bhaskar Bhat: S. Balasubramanian, *The Art of Business Leadership*, Response Books, New Delhi, 2007, p 157

Bill Hewlett & David Packard: David Packard, *The HP Way*, Harper Collins, New York, 1995, pp 135–136

**Walk around**

Gregg Steinhafel: http://marketplace.publicradio.org/display/web/2009/05/20/ pm_corner_office_steinhafel_transcript/

Dow Jones Executive: John P. Kotter, *A Force for Change, The Free Press*, Macmillan Inc, NY, 1990, p 123

**Work with the team you have**

Louis Gerstner: Louis V. Gerstner, Jr., *Who says elephants can't dance?* Harper Collins, New York, 2002, pp 73–74

Robert Mondavi: Lucinda Watson, *How they achieved*, John Wiley & Sons, Inc, New York, 2001, p 171

## 4. You and the organization

**Be diplomatic**

Bill Hewlett: David Packard, *The HP Way*, Harper Collins, New York, 1995, p 100

Marshall Goldsmith: Marshall Goldsmith, *What got you here won't get you there*, Profile Books, London, 2008, p 48

**Be meritocratic**

Walter Wriston: http://www.entrepreneur.com/tradejournals/article/97892559. html

Anne Mulcahy: http://www.nytimes.com/2009/03/22/business/22corner. html?pagewanted=2

Carly Fiorina: Tough Choices, Nicholas Brealey, Boston, 2006, p 234

**Create an entrepreneurial culture**

William Weldon: http://www.knowledgeatwharton.com.cn/index.cfm?fa=viewArt icle&articleID=1862

Carol Barz: http://www.the-chiefexecutive.com/features/feature52759/

James Dyson: Alan Leighton, On Leadership, Random House Business Books, London, 2007, p 11

**Cut down on meetings**

Alan Leighton: Alan Leighton, *On Leadership*, Random House Business Books, London, 2007, p 93

Don Birch: http://www.etravelblackboardasia.com/article.asp?id=67067&nav=80

**Drive the culture right through the organization**

Sir Stuart Hampson: Alan Leighton, *On Leadership*, Random House Business Books, London, 2007, p 37

**Encourage diversity**

Gary Hamel: Gary Hamel, *The Future of Management*, Harvard Business School Publishing, Boston MA, USA, 2007, p 159

Stuart Miller: Frans Johansson, *The Medici Effect*, Harvard Business School Publishing, Boston MA, USA, 2004, p 80

**Encourage innovation**

Whirlpool innovation initiative: http://www.allbusiness.com/public-administration/administration-human/3896174-1.html

Nancy Snyder: http://www.businessweek.com/innovate/content/mar2006/id20060306_287425.htm

Mike Southon & Chris West: Mike Southon, Chris West, *The Boardroom Entrepreneur*, Random House, London, 2005, p 5

**Get the culture right**

Louis Gerstner: Louis Gerstner, *Who says elephants can't dance?* Harper Collins, New York, 2002, p 177, p 182, p 234

## Harness the intelligence of the organization

Stephen Covey: http://www.forbes.com/2007/03/19/covey-work-life-lead-careers-worklife07-cz_sc_0319covey.html

Tony Fernandes: http://www.doricassetfinance.com/de/press_reviews/090518_Interview_%20AirAsia%20CEO.pdf

IBM Jams: https://www.collaborationjam.com

Eric Schmidt: http://marketplace.publicradio.org/display/web/2009/07/07/pm_corner_office_google_schmidt_transcript

## Herding cats

Allen Grossman: Lucinda Watson, *How they achieved*, John Wiley & Sons, Inc, New York, 2001, p 145

Narayana Murthy: http://www.rediff.com/money/2007/may/28bspec.htm

## Implementation

Frank Zhou: http://www.knowledgeatwharton.com.cn/index.cfm?fa=viewArticle&articleID=1952

Jack Welch: Jack Welch, *Winning*, Harper Collins, London 2005, p 188

## Make small improvements

Reuben Mark: http://knowledge.wharton.upenn.edu/article.cfm?articleid=1815

Vikas Kedia: http://www.theceoinsights.com

## March towards the sound of the guns

Louis Gerstner: Louis Gerstner, *Who says elephants can't dance?* Harper Collins, New York, 2002, pp 203–204

## Mix things up

Frans Johansson: Frans Johansson, *The Medici Effect*, Harvard Business School Publishing, Boston MA, USA, 2004, pp 11–13

Jane Jacobs: Jane Jacobs, *Death and Life of Great American Cities*, Random House, New York, 1961

## Not everything is measurable

Gary Hamel: Gary Hamel, *The Future of Management*, Harvard Business School Publishing, Boston MA, USA, 2007, p 98

## Plan for every contingency

Robert McNamara: Lee Iacocca, Iacocca, *An Autobiography*, Sedgwick & Jackson, London 1985, p 42

Sir Richard Branson: Richard Branson, *Business Stripped Bare*, Virgin Books, London, 2008, p 171

John Kotter: John P. Kotter, *A Force for Change*, The Free Press, Macmillan Inc, NY, 1990, p 39

## Practice democracy

Gary Hamel: Gary Hamel, *The Future of Management*, Harvard Business School Publishing, Boston MA, USA, 2007, pp 168–169

## Respect the culture you inherit

Alan Mulally: http://marketplace.publicradio.org/display/web/2008/01/15/corner_office_mulally_transcript

Michael Beers: Alan Leighton, *On Leadership*, Random House Business Books, London, 2007, p 74

## Servant leadership

Robert Greenleaf: http://www.greenleaf.org/whatissl

Colleen Barrett: http://www.knowledgeatwharton.com.cn/index.cfm?fa=viewArticle&articleID=1882

**Set reasonable goals**

John Chen: Lucinda Watson, *How they achieved*, John Wiley & Sons, Inc, New
York, 2001, p 21

Gregg Steinhafel: http://marketplace.publicradio.org/display/web/2009/05/20/
pm_corner_office_steinhafel_transcript/

**Zero tolerance and the staff kitchen**

James Q. Wilson & George L. Kelling: http://www.manhattan-institute.org/pdf/_
atlantic_monthly-broken_windows.pdf

Greg Dyke: Greg Dyke, *Inside Story*, Harper Collins, London, 2004, p 199


## 5. Personal Qualities

**Be authentic**

Bill George: http://www.rpleadingtheway.com/resources/True%20North%20
Book%20Summary.pdf

Dieter Zetsche: http://www.knowledgeatwharton.com.cn/index.cfm?fa=viewArtic
le&articleID=1810

**Be decisive**

George S. Patton: http://www.generalpatton.com/quotes.html

Lee Iacocca: Lee Iacocca, *Iacocca, An Autobiography*, Sedgwick & Jackson, London
1985, p 50

**Be firm**

Douglas Conant: http://marketplace.publicradio.org/display/web/2007/12/16/
corner_office_conant_transcript/

Greg Dyke: Greg Dyke, *Inside Story*, Harper Collins, London, 2004, p 114

## Be honest

Ram Charan: http://blogs.harvardbusiness.org/hmu/2009/02/ram-charan-interview.html

Narayana Murthy: http://www.rediff.com/money/2007/may/28bspec.htm

## Be human

Roger Ailes: Rudolph W. Giuliani, *Leadership*, Time Warner Books, New York, 2002, p 191

Jun Tang: Juan Antonio Fernandez & Laurie Underwood, *China CEO*, John Wiley & Sons (Asia) Pte Ltd, Singapore, 2006, p 58

Gary Hamel: Gary Hamel, *The Future of Management*, Harvard Business School Publishing, Boston MA, USA, 2007, pp 56–57

## Be passionate

Sir Richard Branson: Richard Branson, *Business Stripped Bare*, Virgin Books, London, 2008, pp 4–5

Allen Grossman: Lucinda Watson, *How they achieved*, John Wiley & Sons, Inc, New York, 2001, p 143

Robert Mondavi: Lucinda Watson, *How they achieved*, John Wiley & Sons, Inc, New York, 2001, p 171

## Confidence and humility

Rudolph Giuliani: Rudolph W. Giuliani, *Leadership*, Time Warner Books, New York, 2002, pp 226–227

John Chen: Lucinda Watson, *How they achieved*, John Wiley & Sons, Inc, New York, 2001, p 21

Steve Schneider: Juan Antonio Fernandez & Laurie Underwood, *China CEO*, John Wiley & Sons (Asia) Pte Ltd, Singapore, 2006, p 15

### Stay alert

John Sculley: Lucinda Watson, *How they achieved*, John Wiley & Sons, Inc, New York, 2001, p 187

Jonathan Schwartz: http://www.sfgate.com/cgi-bin/article.cgi?f=/c/a/2006/12/15/ BUGPDMQ1T956.DTL&hw=Sun+CEO+emerges&sn=001&sc=1000

## 6. Personal Behavior

### Follow your instincts

Iowa Gambling Task: Johan Lehrer, *The decisive moment*, Canongate Books Ltd, Edinburgh, 2009, pp 50–52

Sir Richard Branson: Richard Branson, *Business Stripped Bare*, Virgin Books, London, 2008, p 166

Dame Anita Roddick: Anita Roddick, *Business as unusual*, Thorsons (HarperCollinsPublishers), 2000, p 155

### Listen, learn and act

Wu Xiaobing: http://www.knowledgeatwharton.com.cn/index.cfm?fa=viewArticle &articleID=1968

Alan Mulally: http://marketplace.publicradio.org/display/web/2008/01/15/corner_ office_mulally_transcript/

### Say sorry sometimes

Marshall Goldsmith: Marshall Goldsmith, *What got you here won't get you there*, Profile Books, London, 2008, p 136

### Set a good example

Sir John Harvey-Jones: John Harvey-Jones, *Making it Happen: Reflections on Leadership*, William Collins, London, 1988, p 100

Reuben Mark: http://knowledge.wharton.upenn.edu/article.cfm?articleid=1815

**Stick to the strategy**

Narayana Murthy: http://www.rediff.com/money/2007/may/28bspec.htm

Lui Chuanzhi: http://www.knowledgeatwharton.com.cn/index.cfm?fa=viewArticl
e&articleID=2075

**Stick to the values**

Gerard Kleisterlee: http://www.egonzehnder.com/global/focus/leadersdialogue/
article/id/71500010

Kenneth Yu: Juan Antonio Fernandez & Laurie Underwood, *China CEO*, John
Wiley & Sons (Asia) Pte Ltd, Singapore, 2006, p 89

**Stick to the vision**

Ruben Vardanian: http://www.knowledgeatwharton.com.cn/index.cfm?fa=viewAr
ticle&articleID=1857

Andrea Jung: http://www.egonzehnder.com/global/focus/archive/id/99302140

**Stop being judgemental**

Marshall Goldsmith: Marshall Goldsmith, *What got you here won't get you there*,
Profile Books, London, 2008, pp 52–53

Morgan McCall: Morgan W. McCall, *High Flyers*, Developing the next generation
of leaders, Harvard Business School Press, Harvard, 1998, p 40

**Use symbols**

President Franklin D. Roosevelt: Lend Lease: http://docs.fdrlibrary.marist.edu/
odllpc2.html; War Bonds: http://www.mhric.org/fdr/chat26.html

## 7. Personal development

### Focus on the wildly important

Stephen Covey: http://www.forbes.com/2007/03/19/covey-work-life-lead-careers-worklife07-cz_sc_0319covey.html

Martha Lane Fox: Alan Leighton, *On Leadership*, Random House Business Books, London, 2007, pp 92–93

### Get a good PA

Ken Davenport: http://www.forbes.com/2009/09/16/creativity-freedom-ceo-leadership-ceonetwork-managing.html

Vanessa Cameron: email exchange with author April 2010

### Get a life

Tom Stern: http://www.amanet.org/training/articles/An-Interview-with-Recovering-CEO-Dad-Tom-Stern.aspx

Sharon McDowell-Larsen: http://www.forbes.com/2009/09/30/executive-job-stress-leadership-ceonetwork-ccl.html

### Get out of the limelight

Marshall Goldsmith quotation: Marshall Goldsmith, *What got you here won't get you there*, Profile Books, London, 2008, p48

Other Marshall Goldsmith references: Marshall Goldsmith, What got you here won't get you there, Profile Books, London 2008: 'Winning too much' pp 45–48; 'Telling the world how smart we are' pp 59–62; 'The excessive need to be me' pp 96–98

### Good enough

Sir John Harvey-Jones: John Harvey-Jones, *Making it Happen: Reflections on Leadership*, William Collins, London, 1988, p 25

Mike Southon & Chris West: Mike Southon, *Chris West, The Boardroom Entrepreneur*, Random House, London, 2005, pp 57–58

John Patrick & David Grossman, IBM: http://patrickweb.com/inthenews/stories/wakeup.html

## Keep a sense of burning urgency

Fred Hassan: http://www.pharmaceutical-manufacturingnews.com/news-315-meetthebosstv-fredhassan-scheringplough-merck-news1.html

Bill Gates: James Wallace, Jim Erickson, *Hard Drive*, John Wiley & Sons, New York, 1992

## Keep fit

Sharon McDowell-Larsen: http://www.forbes.com/2009/09/30/executive-job-stress-leadership-ceonetwork-ccl.html

## Know the detail

Ram Charan: http://blogs.harvardbusiness.org/hmu/2009/02/ram-charan-interview.html

Frank Zhou: http://www.knowledgeatwharton.com.cn/index.cfm?fa=viewArticle&articleID=1952

## Learn from failure

John Chen: Lucinda Watson, *How they achieved*, John Wiley & Sons, Inc, New York, 2001, p 25

Eric Schmidt: http://marketplace.publicradio.org/display/web/2009/07/07/pm_corner_office_google_schmidt_transcript/

## Manage your time

Naj Al-Awadhi: http://www.knowledgeatwharton.com.cn/index.cfm?fa=viewArticle&articleID=2014

Peter Drucker: Peter Drucker, *The Effective Executive*, Butterworth-Heinemann (Elsevier) Oxford, 2007, p 28, pp 34–45

## Quick wins

Alan Leighton: Alan Leighton, *On Leadership*, Random House Business Books, London, 2007, p xii

Mark E. Van Buren, Todd Safferstone: http://hbr.org/2009/01/the-quick-wins-paradox/es

## Recognize people

Emperor Napoleon Bonaparte: Madame de Rémusat, http://www.napoleon-series.org/research/napoleon/c_description.html

## Reinvent yourself

Andrea Jung: http://www.egonzehnder.com/global/focus/archive/id/99302140

Wu Xiaobing: http://www.knowledgeatwharton.com.cn/index.cfm?fa=viewArticle&articleID=1968

## Say no to distractions

Jacob Wallenberg: http://www.egonzehnder.com/global/focus/leadersdialogue/article/id/54300789

Brenda Barnes: http://workingmoms.about.com/od/executiveopportunities/a/PaidInternships.htm

## Think laterally

Frans Johansson: Frans Johansson, *The Medici Effect*, Harvard Business School Publishing, Boston MA, USA, 2004, pp 39–40, p 50, pp 53–57

## 8. You and the outside world

### Assume the worst

Jack Welch: Jack Welch, *Winning*, Harper Collins, London 2005, p 149

Ram Charan: http://blogs.harvardbusiness.org/hmu/2009/02/ram-charan-interview.html

### Attract and encourage talent

Ruben Vardanian: http://www.knowledgeatwharton.com.cn/index.cfm?fa=viewArticle&articleID=1857

Azim Premji: http://knowledge.wharton.upenn.edu/article.cfm?articleid=1439

### Be accountable

Lee Iacocca: Lee Iacocca, *Iacocca, An Autobiography*, Sedgwick & Jackson, London 1985, p 223

### Do the right thing

Sir Christopher Gent: Alan Leighton, *On Leadership*, Random House Business Books, London, 2007, p 147

Indra Nooyi: http://www.cnbc.com/id/19940404/page/2/

### Lead for your industry

Peter Martin: interview with author, 19.10.2009

### Look for partnerships

Steve Jobs: Macworld Boston 1997, http://www.youtube.com/watch?v=WxOp5mBY9IY

Louis Gerstner: Louis V. Gerstner, Jr., *Who says elephants can't dance?* Harper Collins, New York, 2002, p 157

**Make a contribution**

David Packard: Speech by Dave Packard to HP managers March 8, 1960 quoted in David Packard, *The HP Way*, Harper Collins, New York, 1995, pp xix–xx

Ken Freitas: http://hbswk.hbs.edu/archive/1263.html

Muhammad Yunus: http://www.grameen-info.org/index.php?option=com_content&task=view&id=217&Itemid=172&limit=1&limitstart=0

**See the bigger picture**

Bill Gates: James Wallace, Jim Erickson, *Hard Drive*, John Wiley & Sons, New York, 1992, p 110

Michael Beer: http://hbswk.hbs.edu/item/6108.html#2

All website links accessed May 2010.

## OTHER 100 GREAT IDEAS

## 100 Great Business Ideas
From leading companies around the world
*Jeremy Kourdi*

Know how to prepare a deep-dive prototype? How's your social networking? And are you up to speed in your psychographic profiling and vendor lock-in procedures?

In the world of business, new ideas and energy are needed constantly—in many ways and at varying times—to ensure success. This book contains 100 insightful and useful business ideas that will help you succeed.

Written in a stimulating and flexible way, *100 Great Business Ideas* contains ideas with proven power and potency that actually work. The ideas are varied, interesting, and thought-provoking, and some of the best ideas used in business. Some are simple—sometimes almost embarrassingly so—while others are based on detailed research and brilliant intellect.

If you have a restless desire and the energy to do well and stay ahead of the competition and a willingness to experiment and take a risk, this book will inspire you to find out more or develop your thinking along new, creative lines, generating brilliant ideas for the future.

ISBN 978-0-462-09960-6 / £8.99 PAPERBACK

# 100 Great Cost-Cutting Ideas
**From leading companies around the world**
*Anne Hawkins*

**Struggling to compete? Unattractive bottomline? Do you look for ways to 'save money' – but end up unwittingly increasing your costs?**

It's tough out there. Increasing competition means that only the financially fittest will survive. Prices are set by the market so it is up to you to keep reviewing and realigning your business if you're to succeed in making a sustainable living out of meeting market needs. Customers do not pay a premium to businesses that fail to work efficiently and effectively, so you're going to have to manage your costs and eliminate waste.

The good news is that it's not that difficult. In your business there are people constantly dropping £50 notes into the shredding machine (figuratively speaking we hope!). How do you spot them and stop them? This book will give you 100 great ideas to help you get started.

ISBN 978-981-4276-92-4 / £8.99 PAPERBACK

# 100 Great Marketing Ideas
### From leading companies around the world
*Jim Blythe*

**Do you know how to use promotional gifts that really promote? Do you have a startling brand? Do you know how to discourage the customers you *don't* want? Or even *how* to spot them coming?**

Marketing moves fast—competitors come up with new ideas to steal your business every day, so you need to stay ahead of the game. This book can help! Written in an engaging and lively manner, it gives you 100 ideas from real companies, ideas that have been tried and tested. The ideas are thought provoking and adaptable to most businesses—some are no-brainers (which, nevertheless, are under-used), while others are subtle and surprising.

Whether you are running a small business of your own, working in marketing for a big company, or advising others, this book will be an invaluable addition to your briefcase.

ISBN 978-0-462-09942-2 / £8.99 PAPERBACK

# 100 Great PR Ideas

**From leading companies around the world**
*Jim Blythe*

**Do you know how to turn a crisis into a triumph? Can you write a press release that gets you thousands of pounds worth of free publicity? Do you know how to hijack your competitors' PR and turn it against them?**

This book can help! PR is exciting, it is essential, and it is easy to do—once you know how. Thousands of companies use PR to generate free publicity, to win over customers, to defuse criticism and potential threats from governments, and to put their name in the public eye. This book gives you 100 ideas from real companies, ideas that have worked time and time again to create the right impression.

Written in a lively, engaging style, this book gives you the ammunition you need to take the fight to the enemy. Whether you are running a small business or work for a major firm, or whether you are new to PR or have been in the business for years, this book has something for you.

ISBN 978-0-462-09949-1 / £8.99 PAPERBACK

## OTHER 100 GREAT IDEAS

# 100 Great Presentation Ideas
**From leading companies around the world**
*Patrick Forsyth*

**Do you get nervous about making presentations? How much preparation do you do for a presentation? What are the secrets to making an impactful presentation?**

Presentations matter. There can be a great deal hanging on them and rarely, if one fails to work, do you get a second chance. A poor presentation can blight a plan, a proposal, a reputation... even a career. But making a good one is not easy, as a quotation from Sir George Jessel makes clear: *The human brain is a wonderful thing. It starts working the moment you are born and never stops until you stand up to speak in public.* If you identify with this all too readily, your fears and experience will only be made worse if you make a presentation without understanding what makes it work, without adequate preparation or founded only on some irrational belief that you can wing it.

Presentation success can be ensured, however, if you adopt an active approach, understand the way it works, and deploy the right techniques. The 100 approaches and ideas contained in this book have been proven and can be used or adapted to underpin and enliven your presentation and maximize its effectiveness.

ISBN 978-981-4276-91-7 / £8.99 PAPERBACK

# 100 Great Time Management Ideas
## From leading companies around the world
*Patrick Forsyth*

**Do your priority tasks really get priority? Are you constantly interrupted, and do you find fire-fighting a necessity? Or do you see time as a resource that can be organized to maximize your effectiveness, and do just that? Really?**

Your personal productivity and effectiveness help determine your level of success. Yet sometimes, the sheer number of things to do and the pressure and chaos that may pervade the workplace can overwhelm. The road to hell may be paved with good intentions, but so, too, is the road to effective time management.

Using your time effectively can transform your work patterns, performance and results, and the job satisfaction you get along the way. Time management is also a career skill, one that influences not just job success, but whole career success, too. Yet it can be difficult to achieve, and success is in the detail.

*100 Great Time Management Ideas* is a book to dip into rather than read all at one sitting (a fact that already makes it time effective!). The book contains 100 self-contained ideas to improve your management of time; all are proven, practical, and used by successful executives and managers around the world. As the author, Patrick Forsyth, says, "One new idea may positively influence how you work; here, it is no exaggeration to say that a steady stream of ideas can revolutionize it."

ISBN 978-0-462-09943-9 / £8.99 PAPERBACK